All
I Have
is
NOW

and that's more than enough

John Chuchman

Intro

The Present Moment

is not just a progression
of past moments.

It is Alive
in its own way,
complete,
perfect.

This Present Moment
demands
My Attention.

Only
in the Present Moment
can I be
Fully Attentive.

Only
in the Present Moment
does the Divine
Exist.

I may make plans,
but with so many variables,
I can really only respond to life
with the Wisdom of and in
the Present Moment.

I thus strive to be
Present
in life
with all its wholeness,
without judgment.

Only in the Present Moment
does
the Divine speak to me.

The first thing to understand about my poetry
is that it comes to you from outside you,
in my books or in my words,
but that for it to live,
something from *within you* must come to it
and meet it
and complete it.

Your response with your own mind
and body
and memory
and emotions
gives my poetry its ability to work some magic;
if you give to it,
it will give to you,
and give plenty.

The sun is new every day
and the sun of my poetry is new every day, too,
because it is seen in different ways
by different people
who have lived under it,
lived with it,
and responded to it.

Their lives are different from yours,
but by means of what my poetry may bring to
the fact of the sun,
— everybody's sun; yours, too —
you can come into possession of many suns:
as many as men and women have ever been
able to imagine.

I hope that my poetry makes possible
your deepest kind of personal possession
of the world.

The beginning of your encounter with my
poetry
should be simple.
It bypasses classrooms,
textbooks,
courses,
examinations,
and libraries,
and strives to go straight to the things
that make your own existence exist:
to your body and nerves
and blood and muscles.

With my poetry, find your own way
— a secret way
that maybe you don't know yet —
to open yourself as wide as you can
and as deep as you can
to the moment,
the now of your own existence
and the endless mystery of it,
and perhaps at the same time
to one other thing that is not you,
but is out there:
a handful of soil is a good place to start.

For me, almost anything put poetically
is more memorable
than the same thing in prose.

Why this is, I don't know,
though the answer is surely rooted
far down in the biology
by means of which we exist;
in the circulation of the blood
that goes forth from the heart and comes back,
and in the repetition of breathing.

I hope
the more your encounter
with my poetry deepens,
the more your experience
of your own life deepens,
and you begin to see things
by means of words,
and words by means of things.

I think
you will come to understand the world
as it interacts with words,
and as it can be re-created by words,
in rhythms and by images.

My experience is that this condition
is one charged with vital possibilities.
You might pick up meaning more quickly
and you will create meaning, too,
for yourself and others.

Connections between things
may exist for you
in ways that they never did before.
They will shine with unexpectedness,
wide-openness,
if you go toward them
on your own path.

You will know this is happening
the first time you say,
of something you might not have noticed
before,
Wow!

Many have gifted me
with their
Wows
after immersion in my poetry.

After a Lifetime
of trying to be
something more
than who I was
and
trying to get
something more
than what I had
and
trying to be
somewhere other
than where I was,
it was revealed to me
that

*Everything
I ever needed
or will ever need
was/is
available to me
in
the Precious Present Moment,
NOW.*

I'm resting in the moment

with God as
Love.

I find some peace in
a Triune God
as
Source of Love,
Embodiment of Love,
Love Enacted.

But,
might that also mean that
God is
the person I'm speaking with,
the one right in front of me?

Sigh,
I'm reminded of the adage
as soon as I think I know God,
I know I do not.

Maybe my Mantra should not be
God or Love,
but instead,
Today
or
Now!

I'm thinking that
the miracle for me
is not walking on water,
but being gifted
to walk on this earth
in the Precious Present Moment.

If for God
there is no past or future and
all is Present,
then maybe whomever I am with
in the Precious Present Moment
is in fact,
the Face of God for me Now, Today.

My drive to write poetry
is something I can't explain.
When it comes,
I just know that it is given out of nowhere.
I try to find the perfect words
to name an inner experience.

My goal is to get right to the heart
of an experience
so that it resonates with my inner knowing.

Before 500 BCE,
religion and poetry were largely the same thing.
People did not presume to be able to define
the Mystery.
They looked for words
that could describe the mystery.

Poetry doesn't claim to be a perfect description
as dogma foolishly does.
Poetry seduces and entices one
into being a searcher for the Mystery.
It creates the heart leap,
the gasp of breath,
inspiring one to go further and deeper;
filling in the blanks.

Poetry does this by speaking in metaphors.

All religious language is metaphor
by necessity.

It's always pointing toward this Mystery
that we don't know
until we have experienced it.

Without the experience,
the metaphors largely remain empty.
This has led to the ineffectiveness
of much organized religion.
The metaphors religions use are usually true,
but we too often defend the words
instead of seeking the experience itself.

The word metaphor comes from the Greek
and means to carry across,
to carry a meaning across,
to carry me across.

Living mostly out of the left brain,
we think that the word has to perfectly define.
But the right brain realizes that the better way
to describe the moment
is through a metaphor,
indirectly.

The present impasse with so much of
institutional religion:
that we have for centuries "perfectly" defined,
delineated, and described
the Mystery.

And all we have to do is believe a
denomination's dogmatic definitions
and w are members in good standing.
This is not working.
It is not transforming people.

Poetry gives resonance
more than logical proof,
and resonance is much more healing
and integrating.
It resounds inside.
It evokes and calls forth a deeper self.

That is the power of good poetry
and why poetry can work so deeply.

When religion becomes mere philosophy,
accurate definitions, moralisms about others,
rituals and dogmas in the head,
that is the beginning of the end of religion
as actual transformation.

Now no one knows what to do with their pain
except project it onto other people.

Poetry can be a life-cherishing force,
for poems are not words, after all,
but fires for the coal,
ropes let down to the lost,
something as necessary as
bread for the hungry.

Enjoying My Poetry

I do hope you enjoy my poetry.

But I hope you also enjoy all the white space
that fills my pages.

The white space can actually comfort you,
reminding you of two things:
First, the awesome silence
–all the wordless thinking–
that accompanied every word I have written.

Wordlessness can be precious and productive
in its own ways.

Second, reminding you that
I do not need to say everything
only a few beautiful, dangerous, honest-to-
God,
true things.

Poetry can be captivating
because
I can say so much with so little.

I am so little,
and I want to say something worth so much.

So,
Enjoy not only my words,
but even if you do not,

Enjoy the White Space.

Despite my religious upbringing
in a dogmatic religion,
I began to allow myself
to experience new ideas
and fresh thoughts that stimulated
personal growth
as they challenged my old visions,
understandings, and beliefs.

It was very liberating
to look at the contemporary world
through an open mind.
*When I was a child, I talked like a child, I
thought like a child, I reasoned like a child.
When I became an adult, I put the ways of
childhood behind me.*
(It took me a lot longer than that.)

Opening up my mind to new ideas
allowed me the opportunity
to change what I thought
as well as my view of the world.
It did not mean I had to change
my basic beliefs,
but it did give me the opportunity
to adjust them.

I once thought it impossible
for women to be ordained.
I once thought Jesus' disciples were all guys.
Now I know that both beliefs/understandings
and many other religious *teachings*
were pure nonsense.

In deciding to have an open-minded view
of the world,
I acknowledged that I didn't know everything;
and I accepted that there were possibilities
I may not have considered.

This vulnerability was both terrifying
and exhilarating.
The jar was half full or half empty,
depending on my perspective.

With an open mind I began to see things from
others' perspectives;
and I could recognize the mistakes I had made.
From time to time, we all fail and fall.

The challenge was to acknowledge it
and then get back up again
and continue the journey.
That is the benefit of humility and courage!

Open-mindedness presented a platform for me,
upon which I could build,
putting one idea on top of another.

With an open mind,
I learned new things;
and I used new ideas to build on my old ideas.

Experts call this
ongoing theological development,
dangerous stuff for the old guard at the
Vatican!

Nevertheless, everything I experienced
added up.
It strengthened who I am
and what I believe.

It's very hard to build on experiences
without having an open mind.

Really living with an open mind
has helped me develop a strong sense of self.
I can respect and appreciate
and am no longer confined by
the beliefs of others.

Respectful dialogue could begin.

Being open-minded
meant admitting that I was not all-knowing,
(nor is a bishop or even a pope.)

Whatever truth I held,
I realized that *True Reality*
has more to it than anyone realizes.
This understanding
created a sense of honesty
that characterizes anyone who lives
with an open mind.

For some people,
being open-minded is easy.
It seems to come as effortlessly as breathing.
For others like me raised in dogmatic religions,
having an open mind
can be more of a challenge.

But I wanted to climb the mountain of life
and Grow,
for which an open-mind
was absolutely essential.

I remember the words of Jesus
in the Gospel According to John:
*Then you will know the truth, and the truth will
set you free.*

Besides,
A closed-mind is as useful as
A closed parachute.

Human beings have always been mythmakers.
We are meaning-seeking creatures.

Animals, as far as we know,
do not agonize about their condition,
worry about the plight of other animals,
or try to see their lives
from a different perspective.

But human beings fall easily into despair,
and from the very beginning invented stories
that enabled us to place our lives
in a larger setting,
that revealed an underlying pattern,
and gave us a sense that,
against all the depressing and chaotic
evidence to the contrary,
life had meaning and value.

Some of the very earliest myths,
were associated with the sky,
which seems to have given people their first
notion of the divine.
When they gazed at the sky,
infinite, remote and existing quite apart from
their puny lives,
people had a religious experience.

The sky towered above them,
inconceivably immense,
inaccessible and eternal.
It was the very essence of transcendence
and otherness.

Human beings could do nothing to affect it.
The endless drama
of its thunderbolts, eclipses, storms, sunsets,
rainbows and meteors
spoke of another endlessly active dimension,
which had a dynamic life of its own.

Contemplating the sky
filled people with dread and delight,
with awe and fear.
The sky attracted them and repelled them.
It was by its very nature
without any imaginary deity behind it.

People did not want anything from the sky,
and they knew perfectly well
that they could not affect it in any way.
From the very earliest times,
we have experienced our world
as profoundly mysterious,
holding us in an attitude of awe and wonder.

The experience of pure transcendence
was in itself profoundly satisfying.
It gave people an ecstatic experience
by making them aware of an existence
that utterly transcended their own
and lifted them emotionally and imaginatively
beyond their own limited circumstances.
It was inconceivable
that the sky could be persuaded
to do the will of poor, weak human beings.

But mythology failed
if it spoke of a reality that was too
transcendent.
If a myth did not enable people to participate
in the sacred in some way,
it became remote and faded from
consciousness.

When people aspired towards the
transcendence represented by the sky,
they felt that they could escape from the frailty
of the human condition
and pass to what lies beyond.

That is why mountains are so often holy in
mythology:
midway between heaven and earth,
they were a place
where humans could meet their god.

Myths about flight and ascent
have appeared in all cultures,
expressing a universal desire for transcendence
and liberation from the constraints of the
human condition.

When we read of Jesus ascending to heaven,
we are not meant to imagine him whirling
through the stratosphere,
simply to understand
that he has broken through
to a new level of spiritual attainment.

When the prophet Elijah ascends to heaven
in a fiery chariot,
he has left the frailty of the human condition
behind,
and passed away into a sacred realm
that lies beyond our earthly experience.

Myths simply express our yearnings
for the eternal.

I am learning to look more to personal experience
and less to book-knowledge.

The nature of my BEING,
which lies between the finite and the infinite,
can only be grasped by a faculty
higher than my mind.

My mind
has a peculiarly disquieting quality to it.
It raises questions enough to disturb my serenity,
but is unable
to give satisfactory answers to them.
It upsets the blissful peace of ignorance,
but it does not offer something better.

Because my mind points out my ignorance,
I considered it illuminating,
whereas the fact is that it disturbs
without bringing light on its path.

Each new idea raised by my mind
is sure to be pulled down by succeeding ones.
This constant pulling down and building up
is all right
as far as philosophy itself is concerned;
the inherent nature of my intellect
demands it,
and I cannot put a stop to the inquiries
any more than to my breathing.

But when it comes to the question of life itself,
to the essence of my BEING,
I cannot expect the ultimate explanation
to be offered by my mind,
even if it could do so.

Though I cannot suspend even for a moment
my need to doubt
and question life's mysteries,
I must let the mysteries remain as they are,
not relying solely on my intellect
for the solution to life's deepest problems.
My life as it is lived
suffices.

It is when my disquieting mind takes over
that I stop living life as it is
and imagine myself to be short of something.

So I strive to let my mind alone
(it has usefulness in its proper sphere)
trying not to let it interfere
with the flowing of my life-stream.

If I am tempted to look into it,
I do so while letting it flow.

I had been led astray
through ignorance
to find a split in my own being.

There was from the very beginning
no need for a struggle
between the finite and the infinite.
I am learning that the peace
I am seeking so eagerly
has been there all the time.

We are all finite;
we cannot live out of time and space.
Inasmuch as we are earth-created,
there is no way to grasp the infinite.

My salvation must be sought in the finite
as there is nothing infinite
apart from finite things.

If I seek to live in the transcendental,
I will cut myself off from this real world,
which is the same thing as
the annihilation of myself.

I cannot find salvation
at the cost of my own existence.
Whether I understand or not,
I must go on living in the finite
along with the infinite;
I die if I stop eating.

The finite is the infinite,
and vice versa.
They are not two separate things,
though I seem compelled
to conceive them so
by my mind.

As taught
by Jesus' parables,
I must be driven
not by my mind,
but by my heart,
home of Love,
which is Infinite.

We must have the courage
to bring forth the treasures
that are hidden within us.

Something wonderful is sheltered inside.
We are all walking repositories
of buried treasure.

One of the oldest and most generous tricks
the universe plays on us human beings,
both for its own amusement and for ours,
is burying strange jewels deep within us all
and standing back to see if we can find them.

The hunt to uncover those jewels
is living Creatively.

The courage to go on that hunt
is what separates a mundane existence
from an enchanted one.

We must risk delight,
having the stubbornness to accept our
gladness
in the ruthless furnace of this world,
living in a state of uninterrupted marvel.

We must be Creative,
recognizing and appreciating the creativity
in fixing a meal,
playing games with a child,
imagining a garden.

Without Creativity,
we will never be able to realize our own
capacities.

Without Creativity,
we will never know the world as richly
as it longs to be known.

Without Creativity,
our lives remain small,
far smaller than we want our their lives to be.

Fear of being Creative
is a desolate boneyard
where our dreams rot.

While the paths and outcomes of creative living
will vary wildly from person to person,
a creative life is an amplified life.

It's a bigger life,
a happier life,
an expanded life,
and a hell of a lot more interesting life.

Continually and stubbornly bringing forth
the jewels
that are hidden within
is a fine art, in and of itself.

Only when we are Creative,
and at our most playful,
can Divinity finally get serious with us.

The only moment
in which
I can be alive
is
the precious present.

The past is gone,
the future does not exist.
Only in
the present moment
can I touch life
and
be deeply alive.

I am at home
in the here and now.

I had to stop
running to
the future
to find happiness.

As Jesus said,
*The Kingdom of God
is at Hand*
here and now.

Dwelling more and more
in the precious present,
I begin to see things
more deeply.

I am trying to learn
to look at myself
with Love.

I know my Transformation
must begin with myself,
my True Nature.

As long as I did not
look at myself with Love,
I was not really able
to Love others.

With mindfulness
I recognize my habitual
ways of thinking
and the content of my thoughts.

Often,
my thoughts ran around in circles,
engulfed in
anger, guilt, distrust, conflict, pessimism,
and sorrow.

When my mind was like that,
my words and actions
manifested these characteristics
causing harm
to others
and to me.

I work now
to shed the light of mindfulness
on these thought patterns
to be able to see them
more clearly.

Now when a harmful thought arises,
I just smile at it.
Often that's enough to stop it
in its tracks.

Awareness, attention
and a Loving Mindfulness
brings me
a sense of
peace, clarity, happiness, joy,
and Love,
stifling thoughts and actions of
anger, guilt, sorrow, and pessimism.

To feel the Mystery of the moment,
or Sunyata,
means to let go of self,
to trust totally in infinite openness,
to what's going on right now,
in the trust that what is going on
is what I am a part of
and what will sustain and lead me,
moment by moment,
only moment by moment.

There are no grand visions promised here,
just a mindful trusting of each moment
as it comes,
with what it contains,
with its confusion or inspiration,
with its joy or horror,
with its hope or despair.

Whatever is there,
this suchness right now,
is the breath of the Spirit,
the power of Mystery,
the connectedness of Emptiness.

The suchness of each moment
is this the infinite Love of God.

If we Christians really affirm that
God is love
and that Trinity means relationality,
then the symbol Buddhists use for Sunyata
InterBeing
is entirely fitting for our God.

God is the field,
the dynamic energy field of InterBeing
within which,
as we read in the New Testament
(but perhaps never really heard),
we live and move and have our being'
(Acts 17:28).

Or, from the divine perspective,
there is 'one God above all things, through all
things, and in all things (Eph. 4:6).
This presence
above, through, and in
can fittingly and engagingly be imaged
as an energy field
which pervades and influences us all,
calling us to relationships of knowing and loving
each other,
energizing us
when such relationships get rough,
filling us with the deepest of happiness
when we are emptying ourselves and finding
ourselves
in others.

This Spirit is a force field.

We are inextricably linked with God:
without the spirit, the body cannot live;
without the body the spirit cannot act.

The same is true of Spirit and creation.
Thinking about or imaging God as InterBeing
and relating to God as the connecting Spirit
is a major antidote to the dualism
that has infected Christian theology
and spirituality.

With God as the connecting Spirit,
the Creator cannot be totally other to creation.

Incarnation is Creation
is Evolution
is Creation.

Spiritual Growth
seems to require going
Beyond.

Going Beyond
means
going past where I am,
not staying
in my current state.

When I can go
Beyond myself,
there are no more limitations,
no more boundaries;
They exist
only when I stop going
Beyond.

Beyond is infinite
in all directions.
Boundaries
create an appearance
of finiteness
in infinite space.

In Truth,
Everything is Infinite.

To go Beyond,
I must keep going
past the limits
I have put on things.

I now realize
it cannot hurt me
to go Beyond.
If I just stand at the edge
and keep going,
I will go
Beyond.

By Being in Love

I am
One with God,
BEING-in-Love.

I cannot begin
to define God;
as soon as I think
I have an understanding of
the Creator and Sustainer of the Universe,
I know I have Not.

I suspect
the Creator is Incarnate in Evolving Creation.
All of Creation manifests
the Creator.

As all of Creation is in essence
Energy,
So the Creator must be Energy.

God is verb as much as noun.

God is BEING,
both as noun and verb.

Creation exists; Creator exists.
Being is a manifestation of
Creator and Creation.

I sense that the most powerful
unlimited eternal energy is
Love.
If so, then God
can be named
BEING-in-Love.

I thus come closest to
Creation and Creator
when I am
Being
in Love.

At the Center
of my Being
is a point
untouched by illusion,
a point of
Pure Truth,
belonging entirely to God.

It is never
at my disposal,
only God's
to dispose of my life.

This Point or Spark
is inaccessible
by the fantasies
of my mind.

It is
the Pure Glory of God
in me,
God's name written in me,
my son-ship.

This point in me
is like a pure diamond
blazing with
Divine Light.

It is in everybody.

Joined together in Love
these billions of points of light
could make the darkness and cruelty of life
vanish completely.

There is no program
for seeing this point/light;
It is pure Gift,
everywhere.

Lovers help each other
see it
in themselves and each other.

It is not simply about believing in Jesus,
nor is it simply to live as Jesus lived,
a life of love for God and for others.

We are called to follow Jesus
in a process of self-emptying
by which we come to realize that
ultimately there is nothing real in us
that is less or other than
God's infinite love,
which is our life.

In other words, we are called
to realize the mind of Christ,
the mind of the boundless Oneness of Love,
knowing that in the end,
Love alone remains.

God is Love,
and all that we really are
is a manifestation of the eternal Love of God.

When we seek the ultimate Truth in our own
tradition,
we discover we are one with those
who seek the ultimate Truth in their tradition.

There is a point of convergence
where we meet each other
and we recognize each other
as Seekers of Awakening.

And what is truest
is that we are called to recognize, surrender to,
and ultimately be identified with
the mystery of God utterly beyond all concepts,
all words, all designations whatsoever.

We are to realize that this boundless, birthless,
deathless mystery of God
is manifesting itself and giving itself to us
completely
in every breath and heartbeat.

If we could really experience all that we really
are sitting here right now,
just the way we are,
we'd all experience God loving us
into our chair,
loving us into the present moment,
breath by breath,
heartbeat by heartbeat.

And we would then bear witness
to that realization
by the way we treat ourselves,
the way we treat others,
the way we treat all living things.
This is the way,
this is the great way.

Learning from each other's contemplative
and religious traditions
is more important today than it ever was.

Religions
and perhaps even humanity itself
will not survive if we stay within tribal
consciousness,
believing our religion
is the only one true religion.

On the surface, our traditions are different;
but in their depths,
there is a similar tradition of the transformation
of the human heart and mind.

Free fall into the boundless abyss of God
where we all meet one another,
beyond all distinctions,
beyond all designations.

This is living in the Oneness of Love,
beyond any and all differences.

By Being in Love,
I am
One with God,
BEING-in-Love.

Nothing
is *solely* what it appears to be.

Appearances are simply appearances.

There is no contentment
in a superficiality
that is satisfied with
what *seems* to be.

The journey *within*
into the depths of my spirit
towards the very center
of who/what I am
to the very roots
of my existence
takes me
to my Creator.

The Divine is on display
through me
by my
Existence.

The roots of my existence
find their nourishment
drawing upon God as
BEING-in-Love,
refreshing me
by Being in Love.

God as
BEING-in-Love
is evidenced in me
Being in Love.

I have given up
trying to find
a contemplative method or system
to connect with
and be
True Self.

Instead
I am striving
to cultivate an attitude, an outlook
in my life,
one of
Openness, Attention, Awareness,
Presence, Gratitude, Compassion,
Reverence, Trust, and Joy.

I sense that
these can and will permeate
My Being
with Love.

Somehow,
I truly know
(by Unknowing)
that by Being in Love
I am
One with the Creator,
BEING-in-Love.

Grief
turns out to be a place none of us know
until we reach it.
We anticipate (we know) that
someone close to us could die,
but we do not look
beyond the few days or weeks
that immediately follow
such an imagined death.

We misconstrue
the nature of even those few days or weeks.
We expect, if the death is sudden,
to feel shock.
We do not expect the shock to be so intense,
dislocating both body and mind.

We expect that
we will be prostrate, inconsolable,
crazy with loss.
We do not expect to be literally crazy,
feeling that our loved one is about to return.

The version of grief we imagine,
is one of *healing*.

We expect
that a certain forward movement will prevail,
anticipating that the worst days
will be the earliest days.
We imagine
that the moment that most severely tests us
will be the funeral,
after which this hypothetical healing
will take place.

When we anticipate the funeral
we wonder about *getting through it*,
rising to the occasion,
exhibiting the *strength*
that invariably gets mentioned
as the correct response to death.

We anticipate needing to prepare ourselves
for the moment:
Will I be able to greet people?
Will I be able to hold myself together?
Will I be able even to get dressed that day?

We have no way of knowing
that this will not be the issue.
We have no way of knowing
that the funeral itself
will be a kind of narcotic regression
in which we are wrapped in the care of others
and the gravity and solemnity of the occasion.

Nor can we know ahead of time
(and here lies the heart of the difference
between grief as we imagine it and grief as it is)
the unending absence that follows,
the void,
the very opposite of meaning,
the relentless succession of moments
during which we will confront the experience of
meaninglessness itself.

. . .

Then,
at some point in the void that follows,
(and perhaps because of it?)
we find
Companions and true Companionship,
A Sense of Meaning,
Our True Identity,
and
Love.

I cannot explain
to anyone
who or what God is.

Neither can anyone else,
though we have pretended
to do just that for centuries
with creeds, doctrines, and dogmas.

The reality of God
can never be defined;
it can only be experienced.

Along life's way,
I needed to surrender
definitions of God.

When I speak or write
about my experiences of God,
I can only do so
in my poetry
with analogies.

Life seems more than
I can possibly embrace;
to live it fully
requires
moving beyond human consciousness.

But I do taste its sweetness
when I Love
and when I do,
I think I connect with
the Source of Life
I call God.

When I truly Love,
I think I am
One with God,
I know as
BEING-in-Love.

Love seems the transcendent reality
that I can engage
and by which I am transformed.

As a human being,
I participate in
the Universal Being,
something much greater than I.

BEING-in-Love
is inexhaustible, infinite, and indestructible
and when I am being in Love
I think I touch that which I call
God.

My view of God
and the God I see in Jesus
is a subjective description,
as inadequate as it is,
of what I believe is
an objective reality.

Being in Love,
I can reach the fullness of humanity
which flows from and into
Divine Reality,
BEING-in-Love.

The meaning and reality of God
I experience
in the fullness of my humanity,
open to transcendent otherness,
by being in Love.

God is Love;
When I live in Love,
I live in God
and
God in me.

Every delight longs for eternity.
Every man, woman, and child
knows that longing at the core of their Being,
even if we cannot put it into words.

Eternity?
The heart knows things
that the mind cannot fathom.

What kind of happiness
does my own heart desire?
I was born; I want to be happy; I must die.
Is there room in this universal scenario for
lasting, eternal, happiness,
for Joy?

All of us think that we know what we mean by
Now,
but – surprising as it may sound —
Now is eternity.

We tend to imagine the Now
as the short stretch of time
between past and future.
But the true Now is not in time.

Eternity is the Now that does not pass away.
A happiness anchored in the Now is eternal,
true Joy.

We can even go one step further.
All is always Now.

Not only is the Now not in time;
time is in the Now.
When the future comes, it will be Now,
and any past event becomes now as we
remember it.

There is only one Now.
It cannot be multiplied; it simply is.
The Now is the opposite of time.

Happiness anchored in the Now
is precisely the Joy our heart desires
eternal, and unassailable,
because it is beyond the reach of time.

But how can my happiness/Joy
be anchored in the eternal Now
while I live in time?

My Being lives in the Now;
I live in time.
Shifting my center of awareness from me
to my Being
means anchoring my consciousness in the Now.

We can each become aware that Being is one.
We share Being with all humans,
indeed with all living beings.

Our innermost Being
is the Spirit that fills the universe
and holds all things together.

This Being is so inexhaustible
that it finds ever new ways to express itself.
I am one such expression of Being.
I am the mask which Being puts on for a time
to play a particular part on the stage of time.

But I tend to forget that it is (I am) merely
a temporal mask of Being;
my ego likes to think that it is (I am)
all that matters.

In this error I become estranged from Being
and entangled in time.
But if I serve Being
as means to express itself,
as a mask serves the actor,
not even death can affect my Joy.

When my time is up, I take off the mask
and retain that eternal-now happiness
which is the genuine Joy humans long for.

But I do not have to wait
for the moment of death
to experience this.

The moment of death is every moment,
the point of intersection of the timeless with
time,
the Peak Experience,
what the Celts call
a Thin Place.

Meaning,

for me,
is found in huggable persons
and touchable things
because
Being
has its roots in
flesh, blood, soil, air, water, and rock.

My Quest for Meaning
takes place in an ambience
of boundless diversity.

My mind
badgered by billions of bits of data
is fully engaged
in making sense of my life
trying to keep confusion at bay.

To keep me from going mad,
my mind has been gifted
with an ability
for organizing and sorting through
the mass of images foisted on me.

I can make some sense of reality
by finding illuminating patterns,
constants, and common denominators
learning about the forest from the trees
and about the trees from the forest.

In my search
for meaning,
I can generalize,
I can universalize
leaping beyond
while
bringing near
all about me.

Affection,

from intense Love
to simple favor
is a key ingredient
in all knowledge.

Moral choices
require the use of *feelings*
as they are cognitive,
full of moral awareness.

Knowledge is Awareness
and much of our awareness is
affective and emotive.

Moral choices
must take into account
our affective value-awareness,
even though always somewhat ineffable.

Poor choices
often result
in separating
intelligence from feeling,
which is a
knowing experience.

No True Thinking
is ever disembodied
or disaffected
by feelings,
which are informed evaluative reactions.

Feelings
may be mixed, contradictory,
or dead wrong
just as may be
abstract reasoning.
Nonetheless,
feelings are a cognitive reaction,
not a sideline eruption.

Uneasiness is often a precursor of Insight,
so try it again,
with Feeling.

Dear God,
Thanks for the Gift of Today.

Though I may not have been
all that I was created to be,
Your Gift WAS.

Though I may not have been
fully aware of it at all times during the day,
I know I was totally surrounded
by your Love
the whole day.

Thanks for
the Gift of Life and Love
and my approaching sleep.

Art
can be defined as
the conscious use
of skill, taste, and creative imagination
in the production of beauty.

Ethics
can be defined as
the conscious use
of skill, taste, intuition, and imagination
in the execution of moral values.

Just as sensitivity to beauty
cannot be not taught;
Just as a sense of the exquisite
cannot be packed into a logical formula,
so too the moral/ethical
cannot be captured solely with reason.

Ethics,
like Art,
is not a work of an uninvolved intellectuality,
but is immersed in *feeling,*
in a sense of fittingness,
in an intuitive sense
cultivated only in
lived experience.

Ethics
is comparable to Art,
because Art that is worthwhile
is to some degree
unexplainable,
and if really good,
inexhaustible.

**Moral Insight
is an inexhaustible
Work of Art.**

Morality

has its roots in
Feelings,
not thoughts.

The foundational moral experience
is an emotive reaction to
Value.

It is not principally
a metaphysical or logical or religious
experience,
though it impacts
all of those.

It is not a conclusion to a syllogism,
however useful.

The *Value*
of persons
or life
cannot be taught
or proved.

Morality has its birth
in the whirlpool
of Love.

As Richard Rohr has said,
There is great Wisdom in our feelings
and
Wisdom is not intelligence.

Passionate Ethics

Ethics/Morality/Goodness
is born of ecstasy,
springing forth from
the Passionate discovery of
the Beauty and Goodness
of this generous earth
and all the life
that abides here.

The moral
and the beautiful
presuppose each other.

I strive
to learn how to think,
analyze,
remember,
and celebrate
the miracle of
our privileged existence
in this universe
and to scream
when it is profaned.

Ethics
is not alien to passion.

Is a thing or event Sacred
because of religion
or is religion simply a response
to the Sacred?

Moral/Ethical actions
can/should be
foundational for religion
whether
theistic or not.

What enhances Life
and its milieu
is moral/ethical
with its mysterious awe-filled grandeur
Holy.

Some religions
presume one or more (trinity)
deities
as the source of this grandeur;
others
maintain that focusing on a god
limits our sense of wonder,
detracting from appreciation of
the miracle of life.

If the Sacred
depends on a belief in God
or not,
ethical/moral experiences in life
are Holy.

The Freedom of Insecurity

I asked myself
why, at this stage of life,
do I keep thrusting myself
into the uncertainty
of offering workshops
on grief, caregiving, and spiritual growth,
knowing that doing so
always carries some stress, apprehension,
and anxiety.

A reality of aging
is that many expectations
settle into a finite number of fulfillments,
many aspirations
settle into steady certitudes,
a broad range of potential movements
settle into a narrow band of habitual
movements,
many possibilities
are sorted through, discarded, and edited
down to a routine of actualities.

A reality of senior adulthood
is a fixed pattern of life
without the insecurity of freedom
and incertitude of new aspirations.

I guess I just refuse to be seduced
into the accepted belief
that personal fulfillment
means a settled, secure, and circumscribed
mode of life
simple, straightforward, and rigid.

Offering workshops
for groups of people I don't know
and who do not know me,
is anything but
routine, certain, fixed, simple, straightforward,
and rigid.

They are fully laden
with uncertainty, anxiety, insecurity,
and
Excitement.

Offering workshops,
in that sense,
defies aging,
or at least the
emotional, spiritual, intellectual
RUT
that may come with aging.

So maybe,
for me,
Offering workshops
on grief, caregiving, spiritual growth
to groups of people I don't know
is simply
death defying,
as a rut is a grave with different dimensions.

A Truly Moral Vision
of and for
Creation
should not fall victim to
unnecessary and futile disputes
over a deity's existence
or non-existence,
it's oneness or multiplicity
as in triune God.

When it comes to
an appreciation of
what we are
and
what we have
in this sweet little corner of the universe,
god-talk
should not divide us
as institutional religion
has done and is doing.

A moratorium
on god-talk,
a suspension of religion and religionists
could be refreshing and reforming,
allowing us together
to explore alternatives
to the earth's
social, political, economic, and ecological
distress.

Poetry
is a protest
against
that which is,
an exodus experience.

There is more to life
than pain.

Poetic Vision is medicinal.

The Reign of God
spoken by biblical poets
was the cathedral
at the edge of town.

Reign of God
means
a whole new way of living.

Reign of God
crashes against an inadequate present
pulling us toward
a fantastically different,
yet plausible future
outside the bushel.

Poetry
calls for new habits of the heart and mind.

To pull people out of
imprisoning bushels,
poetry jettisons
customary ways of thinking,
tipping the bushels
to set us free.

Security
in the bushels
is a hazard,
blinding us to a society
reformed and re-imagined.

The axe must be laid
to the root of old ways of thinking;
the bushels must be tipped.

People sometimes ask me
when they read poems that have an "I" in them
that seems to be autobiographical.

People are interested in the details.
Oh, did that really happen to you?
Is that from you?

What I try to explain is,
even if I am drawing on personal experience,
the truth of a poem is actually much deeper
than whether or not something really
happened.

What matters is an undergirding truth
that I think is the power of poetry
and I think that, when I veer from that,
it's my job to know if I've veered from that.

So the truth of a poem is not about true things
or things that happened,
but rather in the question:
are we not of interest to each other?

We are a
Spoiled Species
hell-bent on
wrecking the earth that cradles us,
nurturing an alluring temptation
to imagine
a Divine Super-Being
with parental passion,
omnipotent and all-merciful
who will make everything right
on earth as it is in heaven.

Such delusions
are typical of adolescence;
with institutional religion
all too happy to keep us so.

The symbol of God
as an indulgent Parent
who will clean up our mess
is a bad symbol.
It deserves to die.

Resurrection and Transfiguration
are not *events*,
but poetic *envisionings*
of human potential
to make a new heaven
and a new earth
without the need of
supernal superbeing
who is the way, truth, and life.

Evolution has *flowered* in us
into thought and creativity
giving us the opportunity
to serve life
as no other species can do.

If we don't do it,
it will not get done.

In the early centuries of Christianity,
the leaders of the Church struggled,
not only with the concept of Trinity,
but also with the relationship of each Person
of the Trinity
one to another.

In the first council at Nicaea in 325 AD,
the Christian church was dealing with the
teachings of Arius
trying to define the relationship
of the Father and the Son.

They finally utilized, not a biblical concept to
explain it,
but a Greek term homoousios
which means that the Father and the Son are
of one substance.

The role of the Holy Spirit
was even more difficult to articulate, however.
It was the three Cappadocians,
Basil of Caesarea, Gregory of Nyssa and
Gregory of Nazianzus,
who tried to clear away a lot of the confusion
surrounding the philosophical concepts of
person, substance and nature,
and showed that the Trinity could be
understood
as three divine persons in one divine substance.

They taught that
God has only one nature, a divine nature
shared by three persons
Father, Son, and Holy Spirit.

It was at the Council of Constantinople
in 381 AD,
that the Profession of Faith was crafted.
This did not end the confusion over the nature
of the Holy Spirit.

For centuries, there was turmoil
between the Eastern and Western Church
over the idea of the Holy Spirit
proceeding from the Father
or
proceeding from the Father and the Son,
one of the great theological blocks
which eventually lead to a split
between the Eastern and Western Church.

We have been having difficulty
with a concept of the Holy Spirit
ever since then.

There are well over one hundred passages
that refer to the spirit or Holy Spirit
in the New Testament.

Most people can't wrap their minds around
the activity of the Spirit.

Creation is not a finished product
but is in a constant state
of evolutionary fluctuation.
God is everywhere.

The organic form of the universe divinized
is Christ Jesus
in his love and the effective power of his
Eucharist,
But what about the Holy Spirit?

We even have difficulty
in determining what pronoun we are to use
in referring to the Holy Spirit.

The Greek word for spirit is Pneuma.
The Bible's authors, however, use the
masculine pronouns, he and him
when referring to the spirit.

The Nicene Creed uses the terms, Lord and He
following the biblical terms for the Holy Spirit.

the word Pneuma is neuter in gender;
But the Hebrew word for spirit, Ruach,
is feminine.

Sophia, the Catalyst for Creative Union and
Divine Love,
was the Greek word for Wisdom and is
feminine.

In revealing Sophia's identity,
Sacred Scripture
describes her as
the breath of the power of God,
the spotless mirror of God's action,
and an image of the very goodness of God,
pulsating with energy.

Wisdom is the dynamic image of God's action
in an evolutionary world.

A creative novel, published by William P.
Young, entitled The Shack,
characterizes the Spirit
as a female Indian who is difficult to keep in
focus.
She almost shimmers in the light and her hair
blows in all directions.
The name given to her was Sarayu
which in Sanskrit means moving fast
and also air, wind.

Sarayu was not a violent or destructive wind.
Rather, She is a wind
that catches one by surprise.
It would be like a cool wind
on a hot summer day
bringing comforting coolness from the heat.

The Shack was able to describe in literary form
a theology of the Holy Spirit.

Each Person of the One Triune God
shares equally in honor, glory, worship, power,
authority and rank.
There is not a hierarchical Father
ordering the Son to suffer and die
and the two of them ordering the Spirit
to continue the Son's work on earth.

There is only cooperation and equality
between the members of the Trinity.

The true work of the Spirit in our world is just that,
no need of power over others
and always looking out for the best for others.

Created in the image of God,
we possess the freedom to function as God
does
when we create something new and good,
when we live in Love.

By displaying selfless acts of love as Jesus did,
human beings channel the love of God
inspired by the Spirit,
and participate as co-creators with God
in the process of advancing the kingdom of
God.

The promise of God will be fulfilled
through the work of the Spirit Ruach, Sophia,
Sarayu,
bringing no more tears, no more suffering, no
more death.

The wind will blow
and the world will fully manifest the glory of
God.

Native religions
emphasize harmony, balance, and wholeness
as the goals that follow
from authentic initiation,
instead of merely providing people with a list of
do's and don'ts.

A religion of mere moral requirements
just leaves people in a continuous seesaw
of deflation and inflation,
with a strong undercurrent
of denial and delusion.

The search for balance and harmony,
darkness and light,
winter and spring,
angels and demons
is the more basic way of keeping us
safely inside
the always-truthful paschal mystery of Jesus.

It takes a contemplative mind to be content
with such ambiguity, paradox, and mystery.

The daily calculating mind works
in a binary way.
Either-or thinking gives one
a false sense of control.

The small mind works by comparison and
judgment;
the great mind works by synthesizing
and living with all the ambiguities of life.

The ego cannot stand this,
and that is exactly why it is so hard for many
religious people
to grow up.

Initiation based religion is not moralistic,
but mystical and contemplative,
and eventually unitive.

It unveils the Great Spirit in all things,
and in us,
and then we are able to live
with all the seeming contradictions in between,
with no primal need to eliminate them
until we learn
what they have to teach us.

More aware of my life as a Gift
and closer to my inevitable death,
I do not awake grouchy.

I do not awake with *Oh, God, another day.*
I arise with *Oh, God! Another day!*

Many worthier than I
did not wake up today.
I did.

So what am I going to do with this Gift?

Realizing I did nothing to deserve the day
makes me appreciative
. . . and vigilant.

I opt to forget about Death catching me
with sin on my soul;
(an inculcated fear in my youth)
I now vow
not to let Death catch me
bored!

Faith stripped down
to its essentials
is Mystery;
Doing so is Mysticism.

God is Infinite Holy Mystery
that draws near
through Incarnation.

You and I
are called into God.

When I accepted
the silent immensity
that surrounds us,
infinitely distant,
yet infinitely near;
When I received it
as a
Sheltering Nearness
and
Tender Love;
When I accepted my own life
in all its consciousness,
in all its humanity,
with all its yearning,
(only possible with Grace)

I trust
I have attained
A Mystical Experience of
Faith.

In accepting my life,
I fall into the unfathomable mystery
at the heart of my existence,
requiring loving self-surrender.

It has NOT made everything clear;
(very little, in fact)
God does not spare me
Bewilderment.

But I know
God is Present
where my life is lived
Honestly,
Bravely,
Eagerly,
Responsibly,
Lovingly,
Compassionately,
even without any reference to
religion.

This, indeed, is my Faith.

When I was rigid
and prejudiced,
thinking I knew the right answers
to life's Questions,
I was unable to
change my mind
and accept something
completely new.

Accepting all the answers
taught and preached me,
I could not receive
the Intuition of
a supreme and transcendent Reality
all about
and
within me.

Convinced of my own wisdom,
proud of my own capabilities and
achievements,
committed to personal ambition,
I was not Free
for the experience
of Transcendent Reality.

Not through any of my actions
did an awareness of
the Divine Within arise,
almost unobserved.

An Awareness of the Divine Within
was growing in me
before I even had any idea of it.

By simply
Being in Love,
I was growing in awareness of
and becoming One with
the Divine,
BEING-in-Love.

I try to make
a deliberate and sustained effort
to detect the Will of God
in the events in my life
and
to bring my whole Being
into harmony with that Will.

To do so,
I find I need to relax the tensions
of my exterior Self
in order to move in a mode
that escapes my understanding
and overflows in all directions
beyond my capacity to plan.

I try to identify
the real direction
events are taking me,
based on my own background and traditions,
not on dead conventional wisdom, doctrine,
and dogma,
but instead on dynamic growth and
movement.

Though I continue to learn
from various organized *movements,*
I do not associate too firmly with any of them,
not because of differing views,
but simply because
I have found I can grow more
by myself.

Nonetheless,
I feel
an intuitive grasp
and even an empathy for
what is most genuine
in the characteristic movements
of the day.

I find
a subtle, yet inescapable,
connection
between the Sacred
and an acceptance of
my innermost Self.

Recognizing
my obscure and unknown Self
I sense
a Presence
within.

This awe
which seems Sacred,
is not some magic illusion,
but a release of
Spiritual Energy
re-uniting
that which is deepest in me
with the transcendent power
of the Divine.

Doing so
seems to require
a deep humility,
an acceptance of all
that I may have rejected
or ignored
in myself.

There is something purifying
about acknowledging
my dark side,
bringing my inner Self
back to the Light.

I do not need to
hate, nor condemn, myself,
finding the peace I need
in this connection with
the Divine Presence
within.

When I Looked for Happiness
outside myself,
my Quest, in fact,
became a flight
from the Divine and from myself,
a flight that took me
farther and farther away
from
Reality.

In seeking Joy
outside myself,
I gave up my freedom
to enter my own Home,
a sanctuary
of
God.

I needed to
recover
myself,
salvage my dignity,
recollect my wits,
and return to my
True Identity,
One with my Creator.

I needed to
Be in Love,
to Be Love,
as
God is BEING-in-Love.

Truth

is not something
forced upon life
by way of dogma and doctrine,
but something which
life, itself, provides
for any disposed to receive it.

Our task in life
is to dissociate ourselves
from hierarchies
that provide clear-cut infallible dogmas,
and to distrust such doctrines,
not in a spirit of negativism and rejection,
but rather by
trusting life, itself,
nature,
and the Divine
about and within us.

Those that claim to occupy
the place of God
have shown themselves to be
the blindest,
cruelest,
pettiest,
and most ridiculous
of all the false gods.

God
is
BEING-in-Love
and
I am one with God
by
Being in Love.

I am
because
LOVE IS.

I consider my writing
an essential part of the way
in which I deal with life.

I am simply a derivative poet;
that is,
I learn whatever I can
from whomever I can.

I borrow heavily from those I read,
because I take those I read seriously.

Reading is part of my life experiences
upon which
I base most of my poetry.

I don't apologize for being derivative
as it has never been my interest
to develop a unique poetic personality.

My poetry, in fact,
affords me the opportunity
to move beyond the boundaries
of personality.

Readers of my books
may learn
about my experiences,
what I think is important,
as well as something about me,
but in doing so
I sincerely hope
they learn something
about
themselves.

Do not to put too much distance
between the creatures of the world
and the interior experience of God.

Seek ecstasy in music or poetry
as there is a subtle mystery
in each of the movements and sounds
of this world.

Try to capture what is being said
when the wind blows,
the trees sway,
water flows,
flies buzz,
doors creak,
birds sing,
or in the sound of strings or flutes,
the sighs of the sick,
the groans of the afflicted.

I realize
that to live fully
is to live in Mystery.

Though I live
in space and time,
my True Self,
my Being
exists in my deepest center
with God,
BEING-in-Love.

Whether I am in the midst
of a soft rain or
a crisp sunshine on Torch Lake,
or the hubbub of Scottsdale,
no explanation of
how or why I am being there
is needed,
only an awareness
that I am Being there.

I am learning to simply
Be,
to simply Be who I am,
to simply try to Be
who I was created to Be.

I need not have answers Why.

Only by
dwelling in the emptiness of Being
without seeking purposefulness,
can I Be filled
with an awareness of
the Divine within,
BEING-in-Love,
that overflows from my life
into the lives of Others.

I have learned that
it is my attitude towards
my inner space
that colors my vision
of external activity.

For so much of my life,
my inner life
was overrun
with sound and activity.

In being overrun so,
I abandoned a power
to open my heart
to Wisdom,
by avoiding my still space
of Truth.

Removing the static from life
allows me to
connect with my deepest
Being,
with BEING-in-Love
speaking to me
without words
in the midst of Silence.

The gifted moments
come in the vibrant hues
of a Torch Lake sunset,
the pounding waves of Lake Michigan
thunderstorm,
separation from a loved one,
helping another through grief,
a hug of a Grandchild,
and in so many other moments
of life,
if I am simply
Aware.

As I learn to Treasure
each and every moment
of the gift of
Being,
I am never lonely
with
BEING-in-Love
as my constant guide
and
Companion.

It seems as if
I have spent a lifetime
waiting to acquire
the Blessing of
Attention.

I guess I had to develop
and learn to summon
all my natural gifts
to serve this Spiritual aim.

My intellect, my heart,
my physical being
needed to be tuned
to be fit
for the preparation of
a place Within,
with the Divine.

My natural side
seemed to be
In Waiting
for Attention,
a most precious gift,
a secret charm,
that empowers its possessors
to overcome
insuperable challenges.

Without Attention,
I really did not know myself
(although I knew what I thought about myself.)

Oh, I had enough attention
to move through my material life.
But the call for Inner Attention,
True Attention,
Spiritual Attention,
was not heard.

Attention
is a transforming force
like light penetrating the material world
illuminating the darkness within,
transforming it.

With and In Attention
I am able to view
my thoughts, feelings, actions
impartially,
realizing I am more than
my thoughts, feelings, actions
just as light
is not the objects it illuminates.

Attention
is True Self,
One with the Divine,
BEING-in-Love.

Does the pursuit of knowledge
have anything to do with
the seeking and imparting of
Wisdom?

Does it have anything meaningful
to do with
How We Live?

Restricting the realm of
Certain Knowledge
to what could be proved
scientifically
and expressed with mathematical precision
is tragic.

Misguided seekers
often simplistically reduced
complex matters of life,
declaring that the only real Truths
were those that could be
empirically verified
by scientific method
with everything else nonsense.

Questions of
Meaning, Value, Ethics, Spirituality, and Love
have been deemed Emotional issues,
not susceptible to systematic
rational discussion.

All Along, our real goal
is to learn to
Live Well
without certainty,
to live well
IN uncertainty.

What good is knowledge
if all it does for us
is enable plausible discussion
about abstruse questions
while not improving
our thinking
about the important questions
of Life, Wisdom?

What I liked and disliked,
my opinions, attitudes, and beliefs
were the bricks
with which
the walls of my Spiritual prison
were built.

Because of them,
I was not free
to move inwardly,
to be open to
all the newness and richness of life
and people around me.

What was/is required
is not a passive Silence,
but a highly Active Silence
maintained by Attention
and Spiritual Vigilance.

Through Attention,
my dormant energies
begin to be revealed to me.

When I can witness
the interplay of
my body, thought and feeling
I connect with an
awesome Energy.

Paying Attention
is not easy;
Day to day existence
distracts.

Random thoughts, feelings, appetites
conflict and tyrannize each other.

Becoming more Sensitive
to my own goings on
in Active Silence
helps me to unify my Attention,
helping me avoid disparate channels
that consume power.

When I can be Attentive,
I gain a sense of
Wholeness
and equilibrium,
that transcends
my normal reactive mechanisms
that simply respond.

For me,
conscious Attention
is free-flowing,
bringing my various centers
into a balanced relationship
with thoughts, feelings, sensations
in an equilibrium
of vibrant harmony.

Cleared of my own internal noise,
my conscious Attention
vibrates like a crystal
at its own frequency,
free to receive signals
broadcast each and every moment
from a creative universe
in communication with
all creatures.

But Lo and behold,
Pure Attention
is not mine,
does not originate entirely
within me.

Its source
is Mystery
and I must simply be
at its service,
preparing for it through
Active Stillness.

Attention
is not just receiving;
It is also
Transmitting!

Just as I am vivified
by an infusion of universal vibrations
from the Creator,
my conscious Attention
enables the upward transmission
of energies
sustaining the universe.

A lack of Attention
closes down
this two-way communication
and my mind alone
cannot maintain it.

Active Silence
allows my Attention
to serve
its cosmological function.

Stop
giving up your own personal
Ambiguity
for *their* version of
Certainty!

It's *Your* Path;
Even though you don't know
where it leads,
Take it!

Your *Ambiguity*
is more real
than their certainty
will ever be.

I cannot make myself
Let Go
because it is not a process in and of itself.

Letting Go
it is the result of my earlier actions.

In the same way that the garden grows
from our having tilled, fertilized, and watered,
Letting Go is the fruit of
Awareness, Acknowledgement, and
Acceptance.

It is within the nature of all things to move on;
however, there is a clinginess to
my human condition
that often seeks to delay this inevitability.

If I Let Go of my need to Let Go,
simply paying attention to what is happening
now,
life will move on;

I cannot stop it.

Sharing Tears,
there is a depth of Communion
that tops words.

Sharing Laughter,
there is a depth of Communion
that tops solemnity.

Seeking personal and communal wholeness,
a wholeness that embraces the tragic
and the comic,
the darkness and the light,
the odd couple of Tears and Laughter
can help take me there.

Jesus never expected anyone
to rely on any authority at all,
His
or that of others.

He never appealed to
the authority of the rabbinical tradition
or even Scripture itself.

His teaching of the Truth
is direct
and unmediated.

Jesus never claimed to be a Prophet,
nor did He claim a special prophetic calling.

People were expected to see
the Truth
that He was doing and saying
without relying on any authority at all.

Jesus
appealed to the Authority
of Truth itself.

He did not expect others
to obey Him,
only to Obey the Truth,
to live Truthfully.

The Power
of Jesus' words
is the Power of
Truth itself.

The Secret of Jesus'
infallible insight
and unshakable convictions
is an unfailing experience of solidarity
with God,
revealing itself
as an experience of solidarity
with humanity and creation,
making Him a truly liberated man,
courageous, fearless, independent, hopeful,
and truthful,
worthy, indeed, of our *emulation*.

Jesus
was a man
of extraordinary independence,
immense courage,
and unparalleled authenticity,
a man defying explanation.

*But to deny Him of His Humanity
is to deprive Him of His Greatness.*

Jesus differed radically
from everyone else of His time
when group conformity
was the only measure of truth and virtue.

The hierarchy of His time
did not impress Jesus;
differing from them
without hesitation
even though they were far more
knowledgeable
<u>about the law.</u>

For Jesus,
**no tradition was too sacred to be questioned,
no authority too great to be contradicted,
no assumption too fundamental to be changed.**

Jesus rebelled
because of the courage of His convictions,
independent of others
because of His Positive Insight
which made dependency superfluous.

Jesus did not fear scandal,
mixing socially with sinners,
enjoying their company,
disregarding the seriousness of sins.

Jesus did NOTHING
for the sake of even a modicum
of prestige,
seeking no one's approval.

His friendship with Women,
even prostitutes
would have ruined whatever reputation
any other might seek.

Even His enemies
labeled Him
Honest and Fearless.

And Jesus called Himself
Son of Man,
not as any kind of special title,
simply underlying His Humanity.

God inhabits all creation
from the very beginning.
Genesis 1:9-31 makes this rather clear.

All our distinctions are merely mental
and therefore deceptive.

Religion greatly underemphasizes
any internal, natural resonance
between humans and God.
This gives the clergy a job!

Clergy remind us that we are intrinsically
disordered or sinful
which then allows them to just happen to have
the perfect solution.

It is like the vacuum cleaner salesman
first pouring dirt on your floor,
so he can show you
how well his little Hoover works.
As if the meaning of the universe or creation
could start with a foundational problem!

Christianity rarely emphasizes the importance,
the plausibility, or the power
of inner spiritual experience.

Catholics are to believe the pope, the bishops,
and the priests.
Protestants are to believe the Bible.

But they're both the same game.
It's all about trusting something
that is outside of us.

When this is encouraged,
there is little deep conviction or passion,
but only hard-headed and often arrogant
belief
which then feels like a game of pretend
both to the believer
and to those who observe such people.

Clergy give people answers
that are extrinsic to the soul
and to anything we know from the inside out.
Holiness is largely a matter of intellect and will,
instead of an inner trust
or any inner dialogue of love.

The one with the most willpower wins,
and the one who understands things the best
is the beloved of God,
the opposite of most Biblical heroes.

Religion keeps us gazing
at our own compliance
instead of searching for the Divine in us
and in all things.

We must begin with a foundational *YES*
to who we are and to what is.
This is the primary function of a *mature* religion.

It creates the bedrock foundation
for all effective faith.
We must begin with original blessing
and not original sin.

If we begin with the negative or a problem,
the whole journey remains largely
a negative problem-solving exercise.

If we begin with the positive,
and get the issue of core identity
absolutely clear,
instead of endless moralisms
about who is in and who is out,
the rest of the journey is ten times more natural,
more beautiful,
more joyful
and all-inclusive.

What else should the spiritual journey be?

Clergy have become low level policemen
instead of proclaimers of a Great Gift
and Surprise
both perfectly hidden and perfectly revealed
at the heart of all creation.

When we can see our connection with others
before emphasizing our differences,
We will be much happier,
and it will be a much happier world, too.

Karma,
rightly understood,
creates responsible and self-actualized people
instead of fear-based people.

Your choices matter now!

Threats of punishment
or promises of candy later
create perpetual adolescents
and very well-disguised narcissism
at every level of Christianity.

In childhood,
I began to think of God
as some supernatural being
separate and distinct from the universe,
a supreme being
who had created the universe a long time ago.

In addition to being the creator,
God was also the supreme authority figure
who had revealed how we should live
and what we should believe.

Supernatural theism
and parental imagery for God,
especially as Father,
often go together,
producing what might be called parent theism.

The imagery of God as parent is rich.
It suggests a relationship of
intimacy, dependence, and protection.

Our parents,
if we had good parents,
loved us and took care of us
when we were little.

Considerable evidence shows that
most of us have a deep desire,
sometimes unconscious,
for a cosmic parent
who will take care of us
as our parents did when we were infants and
toddlers and children.

Or, if we had negligent parents,
we want a parent who will take care of us
better than our parents did.

Parent theism,
especially God as Father,
also creates an image of God as the
authoritarian parent:
the rule-giver and disciplinarian,
the law-giver and enforcer.

This is the finger-shaking God
whom we disappoint again and again.

And it is the God whose demands for
obedience
were satisfied by Jesus's death in our place.

Over time,
many in power
used the fear and guilt
associated with this God
for personal power and control.

It became increasingly difficult and finally
impossible for me
to imagine that such a being existed.

Such a being does not,
while God as BEING-in-Love does.

In time,
a long maturing time,
I had to discover that
I could not define God,
I could not even imagine God,
I could only **experience** God
as
BEING-in-Love
by
Being in Love.

Once we are members of any group,
even or especially a religious one,
we have too much to prove
and too much to protect.
Growth or real change is unlikely.

In a group,
we end up being defenders of the status quo,
which appears to be working for us.

Every great spiritual teacher has warned
against this membership of complacency.

The only free positions in this world
are at the bottom and at the edges of things.

Everywhere else, there is too much to maintain,
an image to promote and a fear of losing it all,
which ends up controlling our whole life.

An overly protected life,
a life focused on believing and/or complying
more than experiencing,
does not know deeply or broadly.

People may spend their whole lives climbing a
ladder to Heaven,
only to find that the ladder was leaning against
the wrong wall.

In the end,
there are really only two cauldrons
of transformation:
great love and great suffering.
And they are indeed cauldrons,
big stew pots of warming, boiling, mixing,
and flavoring!

Our lives eventually free fall into both of these
cauldrons.
Love and suffering
are indeed the ordinary paths of
transformation,
and contemplative prayer is the best way
to sustain the fruits of great love
and great suffering
over the long haul and into deep time.

Otherwise we invariably narrow down again
into business as usual,
hooked on the group drug of choice,

security.

The Call of God
as evidenced by Jesus
is a call to be
fully human,
to embrace ambiguity
without building protective fences,
and to accept
not knowing all the answers to life's questions.

The Call of God
is simply a call
for us to *Be*
all that we are
and all that we can be,
offering the gifts we've been given
to humanity.

The call is not to be religious,
not to escape life's traumas,
but to live life fully
in Love
as modeled by Jesus.

Our True Call
is to see that
God
is fully experiencing life and love,
BEING-in-Love.

Jesus said He came
that we might have life
and have it abundantly.

Once Jesus is freed
from the prison of religion,
a renaissance and reformation
are possible.

He resided
not in the bushel while alive;
why have we imprisoned him there since?

Jesus was about
Wholeness.

He saw humanity
from a new perspective.

He believed
that the humanity in each person
could touch the humanity
in another person
empowering that other person
to escape
the fears, religious systems,
defining prejudices, and
dogmatic boundaries
behind which
humans vainly sought security.

He never claimed
that only he could do it,
but that
the Call of God
seen in him,
was a Gift
available to all of us.

His humanity
opened His life
to all that God means
with those that experienced Him
finding a new quality of life.

They saw it, felt it, and
claimed it,
as can each of us.

The Paternal Metaphor
for God
did not happen unconsciously
as if by default.

A Maternal Divine
has been actively derogated
and consciously erased
from acceptable images
of the Divine.

This erasure
accompanied the emergence of
a patriarchy
as the dominant ideology
in the Roman Catholic Church.

The all-male hierarchy
necessitated exclusively male
ruling images for God.

Two thousand years of
non-experience of women
in public ecclesial roles
eliminated maternal images for God
for generations.

Contributing to the image of
an all-male God
was Aquinas' systematic incorporation of
ancient Greek biology
into Catholic Theology.

From Aristotle
and through Aquinas
Roman Catholic Theology
is based on the idea that
in the act of conceiving life,
the male is the *active* partner
who provides the vital form
and originating movement
while the female
is the *passive* partner
simply providing the inert matter
that receives the form.

The resulting child
is thus a creation of male energy
working upon an inactive female partner
with the two radical opposites;
the man being the vigorous actor
and the woman a lifeless object.

According to Aquinas,
because the woman has no *active* part,
she is merely *potency*
and thus inferior.
For him,
female nature is fundamentally inferior
to male nature.

Hence, per Aquinas,
and Roman Catholic Theology,
a Mother,
who embodies an inferior and passive principle
cannot provide a suitable metaphor
for God,
the active source of all creation.

To use such imagery,
would be for Aquinas and the Roman Catholic
Church
to demean the dignity of God,
who is pure ACT
untainted by the shadow of female passivity
and unrealized potency.

All this
based on totally **faulty biology**
raised to a metaphysical level
and
a Roman Catholic Theology
in support of
an all-male hierarchy.

Christian Piety

over the centuries
portrayed Jesus
as meek and humble.

If he had been so,
Jesus would have died in bed
at a ripe old age,
not a victim
of Caesar's maximum penalty
reserved for rebels.

The Romans did not care
if Jesus claimed to be God,
many people did.

What Jesus did
as a man and not as a god,
was to politically provoke/disturb
the alliance of convenience
between the Roman occupiers
and the corrupt Jewish leaders.

His death
had nothing to do
with my sinfulness.

Holy, Wholly Holey

Clerics
are trained
to look Holy.

They survive
and gain some peoples' respect
by putting on
Holy Airs.

They are taught
Church-speak
which does not enlighten,
but does mystify.

They are ordered
to promulgate
unreal doctrine
and
dogma.

They surround themselves
with ceremony,
wearing ornate chasubles,
prancing through
ponderous rituals
to the accompaniment of
music that passes for sacred,
because it is so
old
and boring.

This holiness scam
protects their *sacred* positions
as unaccountable leaders
of their divinely instituted
Church Hierarchy.

Jesus never established
the pyramidal holey structure of
Vatican, Inc. with
pope, bishops, priests, deacons
atop people at large
paying, praying, and
shutting up.

Suspicious

of religious doctrines, dogmas, rites, and rituals
am I.

They tend to
diminish and even undermine
the elegance of life's *mystery*.

I choose
an experiential grounding where
I can engage *directly and creatively*
with the Sacred
resident in the fabric of Creation itself,
not in someone's interpretation and
dogmatization
of it.

I try to live within the mystery of life,
holy and profound,
encapsulating all of my life's experiences.

Religious dogma and doctrine
are incapable of apprehending
this mystery
in a direct and proactive way,
exploiting and desecrating
Creation.

My Growth is not about
the right doctrine (orthodoxy)
but about Living the mystery (orthopraxy).
Yours?

**I have been unable to
Find Contentment**
in my mind.

I think Peace and/or Contentment
might only be resident
in my Heart,
in the presence of the image
of my Origin,
my true Nature.

I have learned that
my Heart
is not merely the seat
of my emotional life,
but primarily
an instrument of insight,
designed to navigate
along my vertical axis,
staying in alignment
with my true Being.

My Heart
is a vibrant resonant field,
a homing beacon
between all the realms of reality,
able to create
a synchronous resonance
between them.

Jesus' parables
seem to be saying,
Get Out of Your minds;
Move into Your Hearts.

Dualistic thinking,
Right or Wrong,
In or Out,
seems resident in my mind;
There is no such dualism
in my Heart.

Stirrings of Grace

Oft, I am aware
of an urge
to act
without knowing why.

In a moment,
I have a liking for a person,
or a book,
an inclination
to give or take advice,
or to confide
without knowing the reason.

In a moment,
I have an urge
to write, read, question, challenge,
or simply observe,
without regard for the past moment
or those to come.

I am learning
to keep it simple,
pliant, and responsive
to these promptings,
these impulses.

In the past,
I would question, resist, abandon
these stirrings,
relying instead
on my own thinking,
my own reasoning,
depriving myself
of untold benefits
resident solely
in the Precious Present Moment.

Responding
to these stirrings of Grace,
I am oft criticized
for acting rashly
without thinking about
all the possible consequences of my actions.

Those criticizing me,
those governed by their minds, rather than their
hearts,
never savor
the sweet and refreshing submission
to the stirrings of Grace resident in
Precious Present Moment.

I am learning that
Wisdom comes
not through reason,
not through enlightenment,
not through reflection,
but
solely in the Precious Present Moment,
residence of the Divine,
for whom there
is only Now.

Through stirrings of Grace
in the present moment
God, veiled and obscure,
reveals GodSelf,
unrecognizable by any
living in the past
or living in the future.

Ironic
that my Heart
acts only in the present moment
where
my mind is unable to reside.

For too long,
I mistakenly
identified my outer self
with my body
and my inner self
with my soul.

My body AND my soul
are part of
my whole Being
while my inner self
is not part of me;
It is my *whole reality.*

My Ego
is a self-constructed
illusion
that has my body
and part of my soul
at its disposal
because
I let it take over
the functions of
the inner self.

I had become alienated
from my inner (True) self
which is the image of God,
spiritually turned inside out
because I let my ego
play the part of my person.

My ego, my outer self
is respected by God
and allowed to carry on
as long as my
True Self
does not.

I have to act
in my everyday life
as if I am what my outer self
indicates
at the same time
realizing
I am not *entirely*
what my ego says I am.

The self
my ego says I am
will disappear
into nothingness.

My reality,
My True Self
is hidden
and eternal.

What I am not
seems to be real
while
What I am
is hidden.

I believe
I can rise above this unreality
and recover my True Identity.

To do so,
I must reject the illusory self
accepting the empty self
that seems nothing in my own eyes
and in the eyes of others,
which is my True Reality
in the eyes of God.

This innermost True Self
has its own way of
knowing, loving, and experiencing
in which there is no longer
a separate individuality
drawing all good and all truth
toward itself,
but a reality in which
God as Lover and I as Beloved
are one.

I am standing at the threshold
of the abyss
that is God.
The darkness, the emptiness,
deep and vast,
is exciting.

Though there is no barrier,
I cannot force my way
over the edge.

Well, maybe there is no abyss.

Yet, I feel that with my next step,
I will be flying
in interstellar space.

I don't know . . .

Often, when I have searched for solitude,
I remained entangled
in the daily events of my surroundings.

My restlessness, my desire for companionship,
my disdain of rejection,
often made me flee solitude
as soon as I faced it.

Time and again,
I found excuses
to talk with people, give workshops,
organize activities,
or just hang around.

I knew that one day.
I would have to find the courage
to trust that in Solitude,
I would find my True Teacher
who would give me the Words
I was later to write.

When I was able to find some Stillness
I found it purifying,
revealing my inner restlessness.

What did I do
when there was nothing to do,
when there was no one
demanding my attention,
when no one was around
to make me feel valuable?

I discovered a desert of Solitude.

The outer Silence
led me to an Inner silence, an inner Peace,
where I let go of all the outer voices,
and began to trust my Inner voice
revealing True Self.

I discovered that one's Inner Self,
one's True Self
is always
a Life
for Others.

It was life-changing.

My Heart
seems to be
the interpreter of God's Will
for me.

When I listen to my Heart,
I seem to be able
to follow God's Will.

God's Word
seems to come through Instinct,
through Intuition,
rather than through my mind,
in what seem to be *chance* happenings.

I am thus trying to form the habit
of acting on intuition
without over-analyzing the situation.

It seems to make no sense
spending hours of thought,
instead simply acting
by trusting in the power of Grace.

I can thus act
without rules, yet in an orderly manner;
without preparation, yet perfectly suited;
without thought, yet profoundly;
without skill, yet in an accomplished way;
without effort, yet very effectively,
without precaution, yet perfectly safe
for the experience at hand.

I am trying
to spend the rest of my time here
acting on my intuition
with Love
as it seems the best way
to do God's Will.

I discovered that
the key to understanding
Who I am
is What I understand
God to be.

I learned that
my understanding of God
articulates
Who I am called to Be.

I am, after all
A Being
created in the image of God.

My human personhood
is not something in isolation,
not something autonomous,
not a Being independent or self-sufficient.

My human personhood,
my Being,
is Gift
in relationship.

I came from Others,
I live with Others,
I need Others.

My Being
is toward and for Others.
I become
Who I was created to Be
through and with
Others.

My view of God
as
BEING-in-Love
thus
confirms for me
that I am meant to Be
Love
of/for/by Others.

Being in Love,
I am One with
BEING-in-Love

Today asks me
to re-imagine my Faith, my idea of Church.

I cannot respond with
a petrified Imagination,
(we've never done it that way before.)

I must be able to look honestly
at my life, Church, and the world,
claiming the past with all its successes
and failures,
accepting the death of what was,
recognizing the New Spirit given us.

I cannot respond with
a petrified imagination
(relying only on what worked before)
or with a fuzzy uncritical desire
for any and all change.

Looking at how new imagination
has come in the past,
I doubt that it will come from
the hierarchy or theologians or pastors,
and certainly not from
endless meetings or workshops.

The new imagination
will likely not come from Catholics
pathologically and inextricably wrapped up
in their religion.

I suspect it will come from
some wild man or woman,
capturing the imagination of the world,
churched and unchurched
spreading like wildflowers
growing everywhere.

Hence, I must stop shadow-boxing
with my religious past.

The new imagination
will not be about fighting the world
or the religious past.

The answer will come from the Spirit of God,
the wildest of all flowers.

I think of Jesus
as both fully human and fully divine
at the same time.
Rationally this is a contradiction,
and yet an enlightened goal
for all of humanity.

Jesus let go of his identification
with his divine self;
he "emptied himself" of his divinity,
but he didn't lose it.
In fact, through this act of *kenosis*
Jesus revealed divinity on a whole new level,
a great paradox.

This seeming contradiction is true for us as well,
but from the opposite side.
We have to let go of our identification
with being *merely* human
and all the humiliation of our human faults
and limitations,
which is a lot of letting go.

In letting go of shame, guilt,
and powerlessness,
I do not lose myself,
but fall into my foundational and grounded self,
my True Self,
or Divine self in God,
which stands revealed, substantial, and infinite.

By Being in Love
I am One with God
as
BEING-in-Love.

It is theologically and formally incorrect to
simply say,
"Jesus is God."
The Trinity is God, and the Eternal Christ is God.
But Jesus is a third something,
a god-man,
which offers ALL of humanity an utterly new
possibility and dignity.

If I can imagine it in Jesus,
I can imagine it within myself.

That is why I personally believe in Jesus' divinity.

This does not make Christianity
the "only true religion,"
simply a code-breaker, a short cut,
a simplification
about what is happening within reality.

Jesus put it together for me,
that the divine and human could be united in
one person,
in all persons.

Hope is Overrated

I'm giving up on Hope.

I have dumped despair,
so I really do not need its struggling opposite,
Hope.

Anyway,
looking back,
it seems Hope was simply
a diversionary tactic
that kept me from truly looking at
the causes for despair.

Hope was dangerous
and misguided.

It was defeatist,
relinquishing my responsibility
to speak out and act against
what is wrong.

Hope allowed me to be passive.

Hope required no talent,
not much thinking,
and no expression of
My True Self.

Hope tricked me,
absolving me of Responsibility.

Ben Franklin had it right,
Live in Hope and you'll die fasting.

Hopium;
I refuse to be addicted.

In Buddhism hope is associated with <u>fear</u>,
in Christianity with <u>love</u> for God.

Hope from the Buddhist perspective
is rooted in the expectation for something
to be other than it is
- a denial of acceptance of present moment.

In this sense it correctly describes an
attachment to success or failure,
which is indeed fear based.
So the Buddhist teaching
to "abandon all hope for fruition"
is a wonderful instruction for training our minds
to release the fear based thinking that keeps us
from awakening to our true Buddha Nature.

In Christianity,
hope is rooted in Love.
It becomes here an instruction for turning away
from the fear voice
(Richard Rohr's "false self")
and using hope to train the mind to listen to the
Voice for Love
(Holy Spirit or Richard Rohr's "True Self").

Here hope lies in the memory of Love
that is discovered
when we have learned to find that Voice
and awaken to our true Christ Nature.

It is at this point that
it gets wonderfully interesting!
Two separate traditions with disparate
instruction for handling hope
that arrive at the same place:
training the mind to return to present awareness
- "the Holy Instant".

Now the apparent conflict dissolves.
Buddhist thought is addressing hope
as we generally experience it,
as a state of anxiousness
arising from wrong mind.

When this is the case, and it usually is,
the instruction to abandon hope is spot on.

But hope, when it is experienced through right
mind or identification with Love,
becomes an injunction of quiet faith
in the endless possibility for healing
that unfolds when we have opened our mind
to God's Love.

So the real source of our problems isn't hope.
It is the decision to listen to the wrong voice
- our personal ego thought system –
for instruction.

"Hoping" for problems to be solved
then becomes just a fighting against ourselves
(so, by the way does refusing).

Our true hope lies in knowing we have the
ability to choose again,
returning from our wandering
and listening to the Inner Voice of Wisdom
that awaits with infinite patience our return.

When hope is rooted in our ego mind and
therefore fear based,
it is misguided and defeatist.

But it isn't hope that creates the appearance
of danger in the world;
it is fear that does this.
Hope, when it is sourced from Love,
becomes a powerful tool for active
engagement in the world.

Take for instance Nelson Mandela, Mahatma
Ghandi, and Martin Luther King. These men
didn't achieve the extraordinary changes
they initiated in the absence of hope.

Their writings and speeches contain evidence
that hope, placed in Love,
was centrally operative in their beliefs
and actions.

These men understood something most of us
are still un-awakened to:
that only Love is real.

This is what enabled them to achieve
what they did in so short a time,
as it filled them with a quiet certainty of hope
- sourced in Love –
that is immeasurably powerful.

Refusing to be addicted
is trying to solve the problem from the source
out of which the problem arose
in the first place.
Rather than refusing the abuse of hope
as the ego uses it
. . . gently release it to the Voice for Love
within you for correction,
and allow that Voice to redirect your thoughts.

Then any action you would take
from that Place
will bring healing light into the world.

Wisdom
has nothing to do with knowledge;
it has to do with
Freedom.

Free,
I am able to use all my Gifts
to Grow
in Life
and
in Love.

I don't need to accumulate knowledge
to gain Wisdom.
I simply needed to move my Gifts, my Light
out of the bushel,
transcending Conventional Wisdom
in my search for True Wisdom.

Striving to find and BE
True Self,
Being-in-Love,
is easy;
trying to be someone I was Not
took all my energy.

I learned that
I do not have to pretend to be
someone I am not.

Finding and Accepting me
as I am
becomes an acceptance of everyone else.

In wisdom,
I do not have to try to impose my will on others,
simply respecting their point of view
as theirs.

Animals follow instincts.
Because I am intelligent,
I went through most of my life
repressing instincts;
In wisdom
I listen to my instincts,
to my heart.

In wisdom,
my life seems more controlled by my heart,
than my mind.

I try to avoid sabotaging myself,
my happiness,
my Love.

In Wisdom,
Guilt and Shame can be shed,
ridding myself of judgment
of others and myself.

In Wisdom
I can no longer be Controlled
by beliefs that dwell in guilt and cause suffering.

Once I surrender
to my True Self,
the Divine Within,
I surrender to Life,
to Love,
to God
as BEING-in-Love,

I discovered
I am Being Wise
when I am Being myself,
My True Self,
Being in Love.

Wisdom
is
Being in Love
making me
One
with God,
BEING-in-Love.

Journey

Curiosity
has been Key,
a needed and important
beginning.

Curiosity nourished me
led me to
Discovery, Purpose, and then
Growth.

As I aged,
I began to truly Understand,
started to have
a Broader Perspective,
learning that there is
Greater Growth for me
if I did not
hold on to my discoveries.

As I shared
my Discoveries
with any and all,
they seemed to impact people.

I did not try to say
"Do this or Do that"
or
"My way is the right way."

All I shared was
where I am
and how I got here,
my journey,
leaving it up to another
to interpret it
however they saw fit.

Others may or may not have benefitted,
but I sure have.

In my soul
is a Light
of my Creator
that carries with it
a Knowing
of its source.

Through this Light,
my soul sees its way,
my path,
the destiny to be lived by me.

Without this Light,
I would not evolve,
Life would have no meaning.

My Spiritual Life
is a way for me to bring the Light of my soul
out of the bushel and into the world.

The more my Light
shines in the world,
the easier it is for me
to follow my Spiritual Path
guided from Within.

Through this Light,
the Wonder of God
becomes visible,
enabling me to see
the Oneness
that belongs to the Creator.

Without this Light,
a direct expression of God,
I would only see
reflections of my illusory self,
shadows of my ego.

Thank God,
I was able to move my Light
out from under the bushel
of institutional religion.

Every Atom
in Creation
spins Freely on its own axis
of Love.

the only constriction to its motion
is my denial of the Divinity of matter,
my denial of my own Divinity.

That denial
silences the Song of the World,
the Cosmic Dance.

As the world became known
as a place apart from the Divine,
a solely physical reality
divorced from the Spiritual,
the Magic was blocked.

Separated from the Spiritual,
from the Divine,
the world began dying.

The physical world
needs to be realigned
with its own energy source,
the life force within it,
by our acknowledging its
Divine Nature.

Our Conscious Awareness of
God in/as Creation
will return it to
the Divine Axis at its core
allowing life to flow
with Divine Purity
and
Essential Joy.

This will release the Energy
hidden in matter,
an Energy needed
to heal and redeem the world.

When I can truly Listen,
I find myself
in another world of meaning.

There, the signs
within my outer and inner life
speak to me,
take me on a journey
far beyond the limited world
of my ego.

They open for me
a door to the world
just beneath the surface,
from which
my soul is nourished.

Before this could happen,
I needed an attitude of receptivity.

Truly Listening,
I come to know
a part of myself
fully alive,
nourished by my inner world
providing the direction I need.

A mysterious alchemy
seems to take place
as my conscious and unconscious
come together,
a mystical conjunction
where I gain
powerful energy
working in both
my inner and outer lives.

Now, I can begin the real work of the soul,
a Transformation (Metanoia)
that will expand my consciousness,
enriching my daily life
with a deep sense of purpose,
Being in Love.

Fanning the Spark into a Raging Inferno

I have been learning
the importance of
Being
rather than doing.

I have been addicted to activity,
losing the primal power
that comes from
my still Center.

I encountered problems
and attempted to "fix" them
with some sort of activity,
by doing something.

Rather than asking myself
what can I do,
I have been learning
How to Be.

By focusing on
Being,
I am learning to
Listen,
to be Attentive,
to be Aware.

In this simple but essential attitude,
a balance returned
along with natural healing.

In learning
to Listen inwardly
and outwardly
to life,
I have begun
to experience and participate
in Life as Sacred Mystery.

In doing so,
I have been making True Relationships
in the life of my Soul,
rather than the illusory life of my ego.

I discovered that
without True Relationships,
life cannot sustain itself,
I cannot grow
in Love.

I needed to connect
with what is sacred and essential
within myself, within life.

I needed to understand
my part in the Sacred Web of Life
and how to relate
to the primal wholeness
that is a direct expression
of the Oneness
of the Divine,
BEING-in-Love.

I now strive to fan the spark
of the Divine in me
that connects all of Creation to the Creator,
the spark that is the mystery of Creation
and the Divine purpose of everything
into a raging inferno
by
Being in Love
thus Being One with God,
BEING-in-Love.

I must begin sauntering again.

Some derive the word saunter
from sans terre,
without land or a home,
which, in a good sense, means,
having no particular home,
but equally at home everywhere.

This is the secret of successful sauntering.

He who sits still in a house all the time
may be the greatest vagrant of all;
but the saunterer, in a good sense,
is no more vagrant than the meandering river,
which is all the while seeking
the shortest course
to the sea.

<u>Good</u> religion,
art, poetry,
and **myth**
point us to the deeper levels of truth
that logos can't fully explain.

Early Christians knew this;
but the Western Church
spent the last five centuries
trying to prove that the myths and stories
in the Bible
really happened historically,
just as they are described.

The Church went backward here,
as we came to rely heavily
on technique, formula, and certitude
instead of the alluring power of trust
and allowing.

The whole point of Scripture
is the transformation of the soul.

But when we stopped understanding myth,
we stopped understanding how to read
--and profit from--
sacred story.

Art, myth, and poetry invite us
into the transformative world of sacred story.
This kind of knowing
has the power to change us
at the level of the subconscious and intuition
because it can open mind, heart, and body
simultaneously.

Children can read stories over and over again,
fully fascinated,
without needing to verify the historical question.
Thus they can live in eternal and always *true
time*,
given away by that lovely and captivating
opening phrase
"Once upon a time."

From a Richard Rohr meditation.

Wisdom,
just like good poetry,
must and will always resist the intellect.

True wisdom requires a spiritual state
to be complete.

Mature spirituality
insists that I hold out for meaning
instead of settling for mere answers.

Wisdom is necessarily and always
partially hidden,
and reveals herself
only if I really want her
and will not try to make a commodity of her.

In Wisdom,
My imagination is more important than
intelligence.

We each have constructed our own symbols,
meanings, archetypes, and memories
that have formed us.

This is almost entirely unconscious
but visibly operative in all of our choices and
preferences;
real for us with very concrete effects.

All the logic and reason in the world
will not change me
unless I allow that logic to change
my inner symbolic universe.

A heart open to the power of metaphor,
to poetry,
a heart open to the feminine and to intimacy,
will leap every time.
A heart trapped in historical literalism,
or closed to the power of poetry,
will remain bored, reactive,
and trapped in critique.

A true symbol is not only a pointer to
a more absolute reality,
but by that very fact awakens me
to the deepest level of my own life too.

Good symbolism, poetry, and imagery
moves me
into contact with True Self,
with others,
and with Everything,
God.

As I fall through my ego
and into the collective unconscious,
the whole world starts becoming symbolic.

I cannot apprehend a symbol
unless I am able to awaken,
in my BEING,
the spiritual resonances
which respond to the symbol,
not only as sign
but as sacrament
and presence.

The symbol is an object pointing to a subject.
I am summoned by Wisdom to
a deeper spiritual awareness,
far beyond the level of subject and object.

Mythologies and religions
are great poems
and, when recognized as such,
point infallibly through things and events
to a presence or eternity
that is whole and entire in each.

All mythologies,
all great poetries,
and all mystic traditions are in accord;
and where any such inspiring vision
remains effective,
everything and every creature within its range
is alive.

This vision is trustworthy
and has a message for my soul.
When mythologies and religions are no longer
effective,
transformation ceases.

We don't need a clerical priesthood
to light candles, bow, sit in silence,
offer flowers, chant,
or pour oil over sacred stones.

Hindu children just watch,
and the reverence and respect
is passed on to another generation;
while we Christians argue in academies
about theories of justification
and who is worthy to go to communion
and that is what we too often pass on,
not quiet worship of Mystery,
but noisy ideas
about which we are certain.

Is it better
to bring change
by not protesting the thing that is evil,
but rather by letting it die its own death?

The Roman Church power structure is dying;
It has made institutional Catholic Church
irrelevant
in today's world.

Do my protests about the corrupt hierarchy,
give it a kind of life
that a fire is given when fanned?

Would it be best to ignore it,
putting my attention elsewhere,
taking instead actions positive in nature?

Do I continue to give life to the negative
by speaking out against it
or
Is silence in the face of abuse
Complicity?

To think that salvation is primarily about going to heaven
greatly narrows and impoverishes
its rich biblical meanings.

Regarding what happens after death
I am agnostic in the precise sense of the word,
which means
not knowing.

I do not know and I cannot imagine
how anybody could *know* there is an afterlife.

Many people have beliefs about an afterlife.
But believing something to be true
has nothing to do with *knowing* it is true.

I am a contented agnostic about an afterlife.

Sometimes not knowing
can be a source of anxiety,
but it need not be.

I do *not* deny that there may be an afterlife.
Just as convictions that there is life after death
go beyond what we know,
so do dogmatic denials.

Denials of an afterlife
are the product of materialistic reductionism:
the conviction that
the material world is all there is
and that consciousness is completely
dependent upon brain function.

Many who believe that today
are as certain about their convictions
as religious conservatives are about theirs.

I take seriously
what we have learned from research
about near-death experiences.
Frequently reported features include
traveling through a tunnel,
seeing a great light,
experiencing a life-review,
being out of one's body,
beholding great beauty,
and feeling joy and bliss.

Moreover,
people who have had these experiences
almost always report a transformed way
of seeing life and their lives.

They have a lasting after-effect,
just as people who have mystical experiences
often do.

I see near-death experiences
as a form of mystical experience.
But they do not prove that there is an afterlife.
What they report
might have another explanation,
even as I am not convinced
by such alternative explanations.

Moreover, even if near-death experiences
are understood as experiences of an afterlife,
most are also consistent
with different understandings:
reincarnation
(perhaps what is experienced is a state
between incarnations?),
a prelude
before absorption into a cosmic whole
(nirvana?),
a state before separation into heaven and hell
and perhaps purgatory?

In short, such experiences do not prove a
particular understanding of an afterlife.

I think they do prove
—or if that is too strong a word, strongly
suggest—
that there is more to reality
than we can make sense of
within contemporary scientific understandings.

I am particularly struck by
the out-of-body feature of the experiences.
If consciousness can momentarily
leave the body,
continue independently of our bodies,
then reality is far more mysterious
than we know.

Like mystical experiences,
near-death experiences are a source of
wonder, gratitude, and transformation.

As I grow
Spiritually,
I realize that
my attempts
to protect myself
from problems
actually created more problems.

As I attempted to arrange
people, places, things and events
so that they did not disturb me,
I ended up feeling
life was a struggle
with every day heavy
trying to control everything.

That just made life
a threat
full of abundant worry.

I could have ended up
spending the rest of my life
trying to figure out
how to keep things from happening
or what to do
because they did happen.

I'm choosing
not to fight with life.
I realize and will now accept that
life is not under my control.

I know it was fear
that kept me
fighting with life
and that without fear,
I can be perfectly happy
just living life,
facing everything as it is
and everyone as they are.

My Jesuit education
gave me many headaches
and some sleepless nights.

Thanks to it,
albeit many years later,
I questioned my belief in God,
my view of Jesus Christ,
my understanding of divine revelation,
my ministry,
and my own identity as a person.

The Jesuits provided me more questions
than answers.
I was questioning everything!

The Jesuits taught me to be a critical-thinker
in pursuit of my answers;
Richard Rohr, the Franciscan,
to Live the Questions.

Many years after graduation,
even after retirement,
I was given a moment of grace
when I realized that
Questioning is a Virtue.

Socrates said:
The unexamined life is not worth living.

I learned from the Jesuits and many others over
the years,
that far too often,
unexamined belief
sanctifies ignorance
leading people astray.

We read distorted-religion stories in the news
each day:
Roman Catholic bishops in Nigeria,
safeguarding Catholic belief
by condemning homosexuality
and supporting Nigerian legislation
criminalizing it;
and in Kenya,
Roman Catholic bishops telling their people
to boycott immunizing children against polio.
in their consecrated ignorance,
arguing that the polio vaccines
were secretly designed to stop Kenyans
from being able to have babies.

They said similar things
when the government began a campaign to
immunize people against tetanus.
Not so holy ignorance, really.

Is something true because people believe it,
want to believe it,
and because they have vested interests
in believing it,
or promoting belief in it?

I ask this question
about contemporary church leaders
and contemporary politicians
with presidential ambitions.

Far too often,
people who reject critical thinking
become slaves
to their own unreflective conformity
and then endeavor to enslave others.
Slaves don't ask questions.

Slaves to the church
consider it their duty to NOT ASK questions
that might give the church or church leaders a
bad name.

For decades,
slaves to the church
(bishops, priests, lay institutional administrators)
refused to acknowledge and effectively deal
with
clerical sexual abuse.

Slaves to ecclesiastical conformity
refuse to question the church's official
opposition to women's ordination,
finding it more comfortable and more secure
to not rock the ecclesiastical boat.

Many people, who are slaves to power and
position,
are unable or unwilling to ask the questions
that might render themselves powerless.

It should be no surprise
that those in control
suppress
the Virtue of Questioning.

What is sad
is that so many
accept their slavery by
Not Questioning.

Thanks, Jesuits.

I doubt;
therefore,
I Am.

Who can I make smile today?

Our idea of happiness
can prevent us
from being happy.

Why abandon happiness
in the present moment
for a vague promise
of happiness in the future
or the next life?

Joy
is not an individual matter;
When I can make an other smile,
his/her happiness
nourishes me.

May I be Free
of attachment and aversion,
but also indifference;
When I am indifferent,
nothing is enjoyable.

Never Isolated
are we,
even in our mistakes.

We are part of
the Whole of Creation,
even if we have
denied the whole.

In my hubris
I separated myself,
yet I now know
I can never be separate.

Separateness is simply an illusion.

Once I returned
to this simple awareness,
I discovered changes taking place
that demanded
my attention, my participation.

The axis of creation
is shifting
with something new
coming alive.

A rebirth is taking place,
but as a complete Whole.

Something inside me
knows the present era is over,
that my time of separateness
is coming to an end.

Though it is beyond my horizon
and I cannot see it,
I can sense it.

Like a new dawn,
I say yes to it
discovering that the light
is within me and within each of us
being awakened.

The Light of Oneness,
our imprint of the Divine,
is being given back to us.

We are each a direct expression
of our Oneness
with the Divine.

This is Oneness
is Life,
no longer a fragmented vision of my ego,
but known within my Heart,
in my Soul.

It is Creation's recognition of
its Creator,
Life's celebration of itself.

The Present Moment

is not just a progression
of past moments.

It is Alive
in its own way,
complete,
perfect.

This Present Moment
demands
My Attention.

Only
in the Present Moment
can I be
Fully Attentive.

Only
in the Present Moment
does the Divine
Exist.

I may make plans,
but with so many variables,
I can really only respond to life
with the Wisdom of and in
the Present Moment.

I thus strive to be
Present
in life
with all its wholeness,
without judgment.

Only in the Present Moment
does
the Divine speak to me.

For most of my life,
I worked with
Cause and Effect,
basing
My Expectations on
anticipated results of my actions.

What took me so long to learn
is that
Cause and Effect
does not work
in the Spiritual Life.

Causality is the lowest
of all forces at work in the world.

What I have learned
is that
In the Spiritual World
it is
the Unpredictable,
the Unexpected,
that happens.

Spirituality is the realm of *Freedom*.

It is Home to *Spontaneity*.

Whenever I tried
to bring Cause and Effect
into my Spiritual Life
-doing something to get a certain result-
I removed myself from
the Spiritual World.

Hindu Scriptures teach us to
ACT without looking to the fruits of Action;
Never Expect.

I have found that the greatest source of
Unhappiness
is unmet Expectations.

As soon as I *Expect,*
I close the door to Spirituality.

I have learned
that I must Act,
I must do my part,
but I am to
Trust
that my action
will do its part
and fulfill a need
which I cannot know.

The highest expression
of the Contemplative Mystical Life
is Compassion,
not pity, not sympathy,
but True Compassion,
the fruit of Love
and its highest expression.

Compassion is authentic
in Service,
reaching out to care for others' needs,
be they physical, psychological, emotional,
or Spiritual.

A Contemplation that resides
in its own isolation
is counterfeit,
unworthy of the Contemplative name.

Contemplation
is mystically a Gift
of the Holy Spirit
impelling me
to reach out
to Others.

Many so-called
priestly and religious people
never move out of
the bushel of mediocrity.

My Spiritual Stream,
if authentically fed by
the Living Waters of the Holy Spirit,
carries me forward
to irrigate the fields of need
in and with
Compassion.

Cut off from the Holy Spirit,
my Spiritual stream
would dissipate and dry up,
or at best
become a trickle,
helping no one,
even me.

**I find it hard
to Love**
a Higher Power,
a Universal Intelligence,
a Cosmic mind.

But I know that
a god created in my image, in human form,
is simply an idol, an icon, a tool.

God is more Verb than noun,
but I can't seem to Love
an Energy.

I know the Contemplative
and the Mystical Life
are a matter of
Love,
a matter of God
that is Love.

I know God gives Godself
within me
as fulfillment
and that I was created
and that I am sustained
by and in
Love.

But I also have learned
that Love is not
something impersonal.

In order to Love,
there must be for me
an Other.

Created in and for Love,
I cannot be fully human
without Love,
gifted me in abundance.

I know that Sin
is the absence of/refusal to
Love.

I have learned
that I do not need to take on great tasks
or even engage in noble causes.
What I do for and with others
can be externally insignificant,
but if done with Love,
that's all that matters.

The greatest tragedy of my life,
any life,
would be the absence of Love.

In the Contemplative Life,
in the Mystical Life,
I am learning to live
Being in Love,
for in doing so,
I am One with my Creator,
BEING-in-Love.

I am truly joyful that
my tombstone
can read,

John Loved and was Loved.

I do not have
my own private reservoir
of Love.

I learned that God, my Creator,
is Love
and as a creature of the Creator,
I have, in a sense, genetically inherited
the capacity
to truly Love.

As creatures of the Creator,
our Capacity to Love
has no bounds,
an inexhaustible transcendence.

I am more than just
a *rational animal*
(Thomas Aquinas' definition.)

Rooted in God,
I am a Being
with the capacity
for totally selfless Love,
with the possibility of
total Transformation,
Metanoia.

True Sin
is not being open
to God's Love,
condemning myself
to a shriveled up life
of self-serving interests,
trying to make myself happy.

If I had kept God's Love within me
at a distance,
I'd never connect with
my True Inner Self,
denying my own profound potential
and fulfillment,
the true Joy
we all seek.

We are All Mystics at our Core.

God's Own Seed
is within us.

A decision to commit
to the Spiritual Journey
out from under the bushel basket
of Institutional know-it-alls
is a response
to a silent secret deeply inward call
to transformation (metanoia).

Once the call is heard,
we must respond,
no matter the cost.

We cannot turn back.

The Mystical Life
is not confined to a privileged few;
It is a Universal Call.

In the process, on the journey,
we discover
that there can be no true theology
without experiential Mysticism.

And we come to realize that
the Mystical life
is not dark and hidden and unknown,
but above and beyond that,
it is an experience of
the supernatural Light of Revelation
given to All
developed in each of us
under the guidance of the Holy Spirit
through the Gift of
Being in Love
given us by
BEING-in-Love.

The Gift
of a Contemplative Spirituality
and
a Mystical Life
is open to all
who seek and desire it.

It is open to all,
not as a means of self-improvement
and not so we can think of ourselves
as Mystics,
but simply as a response
to Love
God with our entire Being
and all others.

Our calling to
Being in Love
offers wonderful possibilities
for Happiness and Joy
in profound intimacy and union
in Contemplative Spirituality.

The Call to
being in Love
comes to us
in an unexplainable hunger
for something deeper
and more experiential
than church rites, rituals, dogma, and doctrine.

Being in Love,
we encounter the Spirit
who enkindles, even enflames us
into the luminous and vivifying reality
of God as
BEING-in-Love.

The mystical life
is not reserved for
predestined saints
or cloistered monks or nuns;
It is ours
for the taking.

Vulnerability
is about Openness,
not only to pain, adversity, loss, and death,
but also to
intimacy, creativity, sex, birth, wonder, and
Love.

Vulnerability
is about Being truly touched by an Other,
Being truly seen for who I am.

Vulnerability
is Being Open
to the sheer adventure of Being Alive,
to the Sacred Spirit that imbues Creation.

In my Vulnerability,
I am willing to be affected by an Other,
for better or worse.
It is at the core of
Connectedness.

When I am vulnerable,
I feel pain,
not only my own,
but the pain of others.

Vulnerability
is at the heart of my Empathy,
for suffering and for Joy,
for hurt and for Compassion,
for loneliness and for Connection.

I am vulnerable with
my Open Heart,
fragile, but Strong,
easily wounded, but capable of great Love.

When I am most vulnerable,
I am most Alive,
most Open
to all dimensions of BEING.

My Power lies in my Vulnerability.

Unless the first thought that comes to mind
when we hear or think *Church*
is *people,*
we are not going to effectively nurture the faith
of Christians
nor evangelize others.

In the current debate
about same-sex marriage,
rather than look to real people
and their experiences,
many who oppose such unions
deal in abstractions.

In response to the decision by the Supreme
Court of the United States
that same-gender couples
have a right to marry,
a Catholic Bishop said,
Marriage is the lifelong exclusive union of one
man and one woman,
declaring that it has been so since Creation.

He conveniently forgot
that Abraham and many others in the Bible
were in marriages
that were the nonexclusive union
of one man and several women
blessed by God.

Others oppose the formation of families by
same-sex couples
on the grounds that children have a right
to be raised by a father and mother.
Once again,
real people are not part of the picture.

From the very earliest days of human evolution
the situation they describe
has not been the norm.
The high rate of death in childbirth
due in part
to the narrowing of the human birth canal
as we evolved to an upright posture
while bearing large-brained offspring
has always meant that
many children have been raised
without their biological mother's involvement.

Also, death, desertion, prostitution and rape
have meant that many children grow up
in homes
without a father.
And, of course, orphans may end up
without any biological, foster
or adoptive parents at all
to care for them,
a situation that some same-gender couples
wish to ameliorate.

Then, there are the cases where children in fact have multiple fathers or mothers following remarriage.

It's about *People*,
not platitudes.

At least,
it should be.

Transformation only happens
in the presence of story, myth, and image,
not mere mental concepts.

A great story pulls us inside of a universal story,
and it lodges in the unconscious
where it is not subject to
the brutalities of the intellect or will.

From that hidden place
We are healed.

For Christians,
the map of Jesus' life is the map of Everyman
and Everywoman:
divine conception,
ordinary life,
betrayal,
abandonment,
rejection,
crucifixion,
resurrection,
and ascension.

In the end,
it all comes full circle,
and we return where we started,
but now transformed.

The basic pattern is repeated
in every human life,
the Christ Archetype,
an almost perfect map
of the whole journey of human transformation.

Unfortunately,
Church hierarchy has turned Jesus into
an exclusive Savior
for us to worship
instead of an inclusive Savior
with whom we are joined at the hip.

This has created a disconnect and disinterest
for both the heart and the soul.

No wonder so many find the Christian message
so utterly un-compelling,
a cheap story line about later rewards
for a very, very few
and eternal punishment
for the overwhelming many
in all of human history.

The Eucharist,
as central liturgy
is suspect in its origins,
something borrowed,
not something new.

Saint Augustine
denied the real presence of Jesus
in the Eucharistic bread and wine.

Nothing was said
for the first one hundred years after Jesus
of a consecration
that changed food into anything
other than fellowship.

The central rite
of ancient cults
was theophagy:
eating a god ritually.

Doing so
filled the faithful with divine power.
Persian priests
prescribed eating the flesh and blood
of their God in sacred meals.

The belief
that Jesus instituted
the Eucharist,
making himself present
in the bread and wine
at the very moment
that he was present with his friends
eating the bread and drinking the wine
is clearly counterintuitive
at best.

Three gospels say
Jesus instituted the Eucharist
at a Passover meal,
making all the events that followed
Fiction,
because it is unthinkable
the Jews would have broken
their most sacred religious observances
to put a man on trial.

(Besides, it is unthinkable
that women and children
would be excluded from a Seder meal.)

John's gospel puts the meal
well before Passover,
and with no mention at all of
the institution of a Eucharist.

In view of
the great cathedrals
built to house the Eucharist
and the two thousand years
of ritualistic practice,
it is no small thing
to recognize
that a Eucharistic practice
has no historical connection
with Jesus.

The Nature of God
has shifted in my awareness
throughout my lifetime
and even many times during each day.

Sometimes God seems to be
a Concept in my mind
with no current experiential reality.

At times
I have identified the Divine
with my Superego,
identifying God
with my conscience
regarding behavior towards a set of rules
for which I will be rewarded or punished,
God as Judge.

Sometimes, God seems
a transpersonal Presence,
awesome and intimate,
an end-in-itself Communion,
God my Lover.

Often,
God seems my Guide,
One whose Will I call upon,
My Helper, Healer, Sanctifier.

I have sensed God
as subtle Giver,
in events and in the environment,
God as Creator-Sustainer.

In powerful moments of Awareness,
I have sensed God
as so pervasive,
that everything specific disappears,
God No-Thing,
Infinite Fullness,
my open-ended identity
pulsing life
into me,
into the Cosmos.

I have sensed God
where I have not before,
in the spaces
between my thoughts,
in the nothings between my excitements,
in the darkness
as well as the light.

I have had to learn
to Trust
beyond my shifting feelings or concepts
of God.

God may have been reflected in my
experiences,
But in NONE of my senses of the Divine,
is God fully revealed.

My Trust in God
has to be Free
to Soar in me Unbound,
free of any of my past attachments
to particular images, concepts, feelings,
experiences,
as substitutes for
the Real BEING.

Over my lifetime
I have had to relinquish
many such attachments
to which I clung
for security.

I have had to learn to move
from a latent image of God
toward an actual likeness of God,
being one with the
BEING-in-Love
by
Being in Love.

Doing so
reflects my fundamental dynamic nature
as an Offspring of the Infinite.

In this nature
is my ultimate dignity,
reverencing the Divine Dignity
of others
in Love.

God is . . .

I'm resting in the moment
with God as
Love.

I find some peace in
a Triune God
as
Source of Love,
Embodiment of Love,
Love Enacted.

But,
might that also mean that
God is
the person I'm speaking with,
the one right in front of me?

Sigh,
I'm reminded of the adage
as soon as I think I know God,
I know I do not.

Maybe my Mantra should not be
God or Love,
but instead,
Today
or
Now!

I'm thinking that
the miracle for me
is not walking on water,
but being gifted
to walk on this earth
in the Precious Present Moment.

If for God
there is no past or future and
all is Present,
then maybe whomever I am with
in the Precious Present Moment
is in fact,
the Face of God for me Now,
Today.

Entering the Now

The NOW
is not accessible by my mind.

My knowledge of what is happening
at any given moment of time,
conditioned by my cultural habits
and modes of thought,
is inadequate
to what is actually occurring.

I am simply unaware
of much of what is occurring,
even within my own body.

And
I am rarely aware of the significance
of what is occurring.

I have often assigned a degree of significance
to an event in my life,
only to discover later
a much different pattern.

Whenever I discovered
the inadequacy of my knowledge/mind,
I either excused it,
or forgot it.

I rarely addressed the inadequacy,

losing the chance to
enter into it,
feel it,
and address it.

Do I know what is really going on
in my own inner world?

Do I really know what is really going on
in the inner world of others?

What do I look like in the eyes of others?

What do I actually see
in the world around me?

When I take the time,
and make the effort
to acknowledge my vast and obscure
ignorance,
I learn
Deep Humility.

Doing so,
I am inspired to a new kind of initiative,
a reaching out
to All that is Other
toward a new kind of Awareness.

How ironic!

My becoming *Aware* of

the inadequacy of my mind/knowledge
leads me to
a more adequate awareness
of my true state.

A key, thus, for me
to being able to enter the Now
is the realization that my mind alone
provides inadequate knowledge,
that I must reach out to All that is Other in
Creation,
and in doing so
attain a greater self-awareness.

For the Creator,
Now is all that exists.
When I become more truly self-aware,
beyond the inadequacy of my knowledge,
seeing myself as one with the Creator,
I can enter Now.

Meeting Past and Future NOW

Having spent too little of my conscious and
unconscious time
in the Present Moment,
I now strive to do that.

I am influenced by my past,
but am also influenced by my future
through anticipation
about what might happen then,
along with any related fear and anxiety.

So, though I know that
the Future does not yet exist,
my thoughts about it affect me
in the NOW.

The Past and the Future
do flow together for me
in the Whirlpool that is the Present Moment.

I carry in me the legacy
of what I did, felt, thought in the past.
My anticipations, fears, anxieties about the
future
strongly affect me NOW.

I seek to dispel these thoughts
by continuously telling myself that,
just as any feelings I now have
about events in the past
will not change the past,
fears and anxieties about the future
will not change the future.

So maybe now I can approach
both my Past and my Future
with an openness, an inclusiveness,
an acceptance,
by simply taking more time having a long loving
look at what IS.

The only moment
in which
I can be alive
is
the precious present.

The past is gone;
the future does not exist;
only in
the present moment
can I touch life
and
be deeply alive.

I am at home
in the here and now.

I had to stop
running to
the future
to find happiness.

As Jesus said,
The Kingdom of God
is at Hand
here and now.

Dwelling more and more
in the precious present,
I begin to see things
more deeply.

I am trying to learn
to look at myself
with Love.

I know my Transformation
must begin with myself,
my True Nature.

As long as I did not
look at myself with Love,
I was not really able
to Love others.

With mindfulness
I recognize my habitual
ways of thinking
and the content of my thoughts.

Often,
my thoughts ran around in circles,
engulfed in
anger, guilt, distrust, conflict, pessimism,
and sorrow.

When my mind was like that,
my words and actions
manifested these characteristics
causing harm
to others
and to me.

I work now
to shed the light of mindfulness
on these thought patterns
to be able to see them
more clearly.

Now when a harmful thought arises,
I just smile at it.
Often that's enough to stop it
in its tracks.

Awareness, attention
and a Loving Mindfulness
bring me
a sense of
peace, clarity, happiness, joy,
and
Love,
stifling thoughts and actions of
anger, guilt, sorrow, and pessimism.

Questions without Answers

My anxious moments
of uncertainty and doubt
have been eased
by my delight
in exploration
and a deep trust in
the Divine within.

My fears demanded answers,
which institutional religion
vainly attempted to provide;
But theology
did not overcome fear,
filling my head with facts/beliefs
leading to
a false sense of knowing,
a false security.

Though uncertainty
troubled my ego,
it bothers not
my Spirit
and
the connection I feel
with the Divine within.

Uncertainty
has become my teacher,
my friend.

Religion's guilt and unworthiness programming
no longer cause me to fear.

I have discovered
a Wisdom in uncertainty,
living the Questions
and learning in the process.

I have learned
that the past is not the best source of Truth
as taught by fundamental religion;
The best source of Truth
is the Precious Present Moment
when I am willing to live
Inside the Question
while experiencing
Security and Peace
in the midst of
my Not Being Sure.

Peace is not the lack of storms,
but being secure amid them.

I touch Truth
when my curiosity
meets uncertainty
with confidence in
the Divine within;
Theology or my need for it
then flees.

Answers don't remove my fear anyway,
Presence and Connection do.

For me,
living in the Question: What is Truth
is to live in the Presence of the Divine.

When I doubt,
I come close to being
who I was created to be
and
one with my Creator.

Remembering

I keep asking
Why I am here.

I keep asking
What is my purpose in Life.

I keep trying
to remember.

I feel closest to the Divine
when I quest for
Wisdom, Insight, Courage and Strength
To Be
Who I Was Created To Be
right now
in the Precious Present Moment.

It seems I really must learn from
What Is
before I can approach Wisdom.

I do not gain Understanding
on my knees in some chapel
but only in
Living Life's Experiences
Fully.

I found
a Source of Wisdom
to be
The Divine Feminine
resident Within
all along.

So I just keep praying
To Remember
Who I Am
and
Why I Am Here Now
with a higher consciousness.

In Chinese,
there is no *inner* division
between mind and heart.
In Compassion,
there's no *outer* division
between myself and other.

The Way of Love

overcomes
fear, apathy, defensiveness, and aggression.

Love is an active process
and as Mother Teresa proclaimed
Peace is *Love in Action*.

To Traverse the Way of Love,
I had to
Move Beyond Ego,
seeing myself simply as part of the whole.

To Traverse the Way of Love,
I had to
See Myself as
a Beautiful Creation of God,
not unworthy as taught by religions.

To Traverse the Way of Love,
I had to
Transcend Judgment
of myself and others.

To Traverse the Way of Love,
I had to
Transcend my Anger
(which was all but possessing me.)

To Traverse the Way of Love,
I had to
Live in the Precious Present Moment,
not in hope of some future reward.

To Traverse the Way of Love,
I had to
Be of Loving Service,
helping any the best I could.

Life Flows

Authorities in my past
gave me views
about things that happened in the past.
For a long time,
I kept those views frozen
as my own views.

I thought the *authorities* had it right.

And so, I was encased in ice.
My projections of the future
were mired in the frozen views of the past.

But Life, True Life,
is not ice-bound;
Life Flows.

Truth is always In Movement.

But the key is
the Quality of Mind and Heart
that I bring to the Present Moment.

I discovered that I must bring
to every single precious present moment
Joy, Compassion, and Equanimity.

What I bring to the flowing present moment
is what brings balance to life
and makes that moment beautiful.

I discovered that I must approach
each present moment
with a Precision of Presence
which, without gentleness and tenderness,
could become cutting or wounding.

My Life has been a flowing river
since Beauty came,
in my ability to see things
as they are
in the moment
and taking Joy in that,
even though
the moment flows
and constantly changes.

Those who wanted me to freeze my ideas,
those who wanted their ideas to be my ideas,
based their lives on exclusivity.

But I discovered that True Wisdom
comes in Inclusivity,
in being Open to All
that the river of life brings me.

I cannot be completely inclusive
unless I inhabit the present Moment
and
I cannot inhabit the present moment
if I exclude anyone or anything.

I cannot be completely inclusive
unless I fully inhabit the present Moment
and
I cannot inhabit the present moment
if I am exclusive.

I cannot be completely inclusive
unless I inhabit the present Moment
and
I cannot inhabit the present moment
if my ideas are the frozen ideas
given me by someone in my past.

Self-Discovery

No one can keep me from
discovering/uncovering
my True Self,
except me.

Nothing can inhibit me from
finding who I was created to be
except my own lack of courage, patience,
imagination.

My journey of Self-Discovery
is all mine
to walk or to avoid.

I must shed some things along the way
and cannot waste my precious time
lamenting any hurts, losses, setbacks
or missteps.
I must be willing to let go
of the masks I wore/roles I played
in the process of surviving
and establishing my identity.

The journey is not without pain and grief.

If I do not find True Self,
it is only my doing.

I know God always gives me exactly
what I truly need
so I DO deeply desire
my True Self, God, Goodness, Truth, and Beauty
in Love.

Balance

The struggle
to balance effort and effortlessness
--both of which are needed--
is difficult.

When I am tempted
towards self-righteousness
by fulfilling all the religious externals
prescribed by institutional religion,
all I end up doing
is reinforcing Spiritual pride.

When I am tempted
to escape reality with distractions,
all I end up doing
is wasting the Precious Present Moment.

Instead I strive
at each moment
to do what brings me back to my Center,
my True Self.

I constantly seek
that balance
between detachment and dedication
with burning passion.

The Contemplative Life and the Active Life
are not mutually exclusive;
I need both
as each flows from the other.

Dear God,
help me find that Balance.

Some Joys of Spiritual Growth

Along my Spiritual Journey,
I have tasted some sweet fruit.
I'm not sure
if they are benefits of Spiritual Growth
or requirements;
maybe both.

I have become more *Open,*
more receptive to people and events
with the result
that I am more able to be of help to them.

Just as a flower simply opens
to the light and heat of the sun
I must be open and receptive
to the Divine at work
all around me.

Along the way,
I am learning to enjoy
the precious *Present* moment.
It is Sacramental,
where God resides.

It is in the Present Moment
where I truly connect
with Others.

On this journey,
I have been learning how to
Listen
with my whole Heart.

Through *Listening,*
I can sense Ultimate Reality.

Another sweet sweet fruit
of the Spiritual Journey
is the ability to
Just Be.

I have become more aware
of my capacity for just
Being.

I am learning
simply *to be*
in the deepest sense of my nature,
my mystical being.

My friend the tree
does not try to be anything other than
what it was created to be,
a lesson for me.

Another great gift of the journey
is *Seeing,*
Seeing things as they are,
Seeing myself as I am, without pretense.

Seeing is knowing from the heart.

It is a gift of perspective,
being able to see everything in its proper place,
allowing real balance in life.

Another wonderful gift of the journey
is *Spontaneity*.
It inspires me to acts of kindness, compassion,
Love.

Spontaneity results from and supports
selflessness,
allowing me to smile generously and effortlessly
at any of life's unexpected events or meetings.

A fantastic fruit of Spiritual Growth
is pure *Joy*.
Happiness comes and goes with happenings;
the *Joy* of the Spiritual Journey
is all pervasive,
the presence of the Divine within,
it seems.

It saturates my being!

It engenders my sense of Humor
enlarging my capacity for Life
and Love.

Though the Journey
is lifelong,
all along the way,
I am gifted with a keen sense of
Peace.

But what I have learned
through experience
is that true *Peace* is not
quiet, tranquility, restfulness,
(though those are good and needed)
but that true *Peace* is

Love in Action.

Join me on our Spiritual Journey
and enjoy the Gifts of
Openness, Presence, Listening, Being, Seeing,
Spontaneity,
Joy and Peace.

Taking a Moment to Hear

Sitting out on my front deck,
Autumn Sunset approaching,
I wanted to simply enjoy
the moment.

There were no boats on the lake;
most were in storage already
and the wind was light
so I heard no water lapping at the shore.

Many neighboring cottages
were shut for the season
or simply awaiting closure
with school taking all the tourists home.

The red, orange, bronze, and brown leaves
blazed alongside the evergreens
and crystal blue Torch Lake,
but with no fanfare.

What screamed out at me
was
the Silence!

An occasional caw from
one of the big black birds
disturbed it,
but the pure sweet silence
was pure tranquility.

I listened.

I heard nothing,

except the Silence.

What a gift it was!

The setting sun turning the clouds all afire
demanded a symphonic accompaniment,
but all old sol got this night
was
Blessed
Sweet
Silence.

Even the falling leaves
dared not disturb the peace
landing softly on the grass
with no sound at all.

No squirrels scurried about
hunting acorns
and the nocturnals
must have hid in waiting.

I Listened.

I heard

Silence.

What a gift!

Was it really as rare a gift as it seemed
or did I just fail to notice it
or listen for it?

So,
I did nothing,
not wanting a sound from me,
a cough,
a stirring,
to end this most wonderful
Precious Present.

And oh so it was.

Choose

I choose a Faith
that does not try to escape this world,
but instead,
to live fully, compassionately IN it.

For me, Jesus HAS come;
I need no second coming.

I choose to focus,
not on an original sin,
but on the Original Blessing,
Creation.

Jesus did not encourage us
to try and get out of this world,
only to be IN it and to LEARN from it;
The Kingdom of God is at hand.

I choose a Faith
that lives in the Divine Within me,
instead of dwelling in
a sin and redemption theology.

I choose,
Communion rather than separation,
Wholeness and Connection rather than
dualism,
Personal Responsibility rather than external
control.

I choose
the Reality of the Precious Present Moment
rather than the hope for a future messiah,
savior, or rescuer.

I see Jesus, not as a savior of the sinful,
but as One who
Unites us All,
Brings Everyone Together at the Table,
Nurtures, Heals, and Transforms,
Loves,
Brings Hope.
I see Jesus as One who
Sets us FREE from religious domination
and
Unites every human to the Source of Life.

Jesus did not invite us
to a kingdom of religious exclusivity and
intolerance,
but instead,
to be part of a movement,
part of a living organism,
not some dead faith
or corporate organization.

Thank God,
the Divine Feminine is blowing away
the years of encrustation.

Thank God,
more and more people are Awakening
and
Moving from false hope
of a gallant escape to
Building the kind of Community
envisioned by Jesus.

The *Second Coming*
I choose
is the
Divine Feminine rebalancing the earth.

Choose.

Days

I had to discover that
Days are where I live.

Each day is precious for me,
a microcosm of my whole life.

Each new day
seems to offer me possibilities and promises
I have not seen before.

I had to discover that
to honor the full possibility of my life,
I had to honor
each *Day's* possibilities.

Each one is different.

Yet, each day deepens
what has already happened to me,
while unfolding what is
surprising, unpredictable, and creative.

Though I wished to change my life,
my vision remained merely talk
until it entered the practice of
my Day.

I had to discover that
each day is *Sacred.*

And as I pray each day
for God to give me the courage and strength
to do God's Will, *today*,
Helping me to Love, *today*,
to Heal in God's Name, *today*,
to Grow in Faith, today *and*
to Help Others Find God, *today*,

I have never received a negative response.

When
my sense of time

overcomes

my sense of place,

I lose.

The Dance

If I can only let go
of my obsession
in trying to think what it all means,
I might be able to hear the music
and join in the dance.

I don't I have to go far
to hear the music.
When I am alone on a starlight night,
When I see migrating birds,
When I see roses bloom,
When I see Torch Lake,
calm as a mirror reflecting the cosmos
or wild as the ocean,
When I know Love—
At such moments,
An awakening,
A turning aside of judgments,
Newness, Emptiness, Purity of Vision
provide the music
and a glimpse of the dance.

The more I persist in misunderstanding life,
the more I try to analyze things into strange
finalities
with complex purposes of my own,
the more I involve myself
in sadness, absurdity and despair.

But,
it doesn't matter
because no analysis of mine can change the
reality of things
or stain the joy of the dance
which is always there.

Indeed,
I am in the midst of it
and
It is in the midst of me;
It beats in my very blood
whether I want it to or not.

I have been invited
to forget myself,
cast my awful analyses and explanations to the
winds
and
enjoy the dance.

Join me?

I try to yoke my body and mind
to the ultimate reality
all about me.

I fix my attention on my mantra,
the Jesus prayer,
or on my breath
or the moment
to quiet the seemingly automatic activities
of my mind.

I try to hold fast my *attention*
without relinquishing it
to all the forces that tend to scatter it.
I seek inner silence
in the face of outer chaos.

But my attention moves from object to object,
intermittent and passive.
It inadvertently tries to sort out
what the automatic activity
of my mind presents.
This attention is not so much something I do
as much as something that happens to me.

The attention I seek is different;
It curtails these autonomous activities
and stops my inner dialogue
and a flow of images.

Trying to stop my mind with mind
seems self-defeating.

My helpers include
impartiality, compassion, and acceptance.

When images, thoughts, feelings, arise,
I try to resist their lure;
I try not to let them steal my attention
and send it down a stream of associations.

I try to dis-identify with content of
consciousness,
while maintaining a choiceless non-reactive
awareness
and quieting my ego with its preferences.

This attempt at *active* attention
helps free me from ego-centeredness,
from blindness
to the more inclusive realities.

I begin to be able to
take long loving looks at what is,
at what *really is.*
(Richard Rohr's definition of Contemplation)

I know that we all share
in the undying life of the ultimately real,
but my *false self* gets in the way,
my automatic, ego-centric, habit formed
patterns of thought, reaction, and assessment.

As long as I persist in that false-self,
by identifying with the changing content
of my consciousness,
my true-self remains hidden to me.

I know that my *Spiritual Freedom*
means a freedom from such automatic
identification,
a freedom from a lack of attention.

I know that concentrated, non-reactive, active
Attention
can transform me.
It can lead to the shedding of
my false-self.

The mere act of trying to hold my mind to a
single point,
the present moment,
has shown me what little control I have
over my mind's flow.

*It is not a matter of focusing on a single object,
for then I identify with that object.*

I learn that there is a difference between
consciousness
and the contents of my consciousness.

Contemplative Attention
(concentrated and non-reactive)
starves energy
from my automatic processes.

When I starve them of energy,
they begin to weaken and dissolve.

When I can deprive
my automatic processes of the mind
the nutrition they gained
from my distracted states of mind,
they begin to disintegrate.

This begins a Spiritual Liberation,
a freeing from the bondage
to my false-self
through a lack of attention.

If I keep at it,
I know
mystical experiences will no longer
simply fade into ineffectual memories
and that
transformation will take place.

Quest for Silence

Silence is a contradiction:

It is absence and presence,
path to a place and the place itself,
the absence of noise, but never empty.

It alarms me, sometimes so unbearable,
I fill it with noise.

Yet,
it is in Silence
that I hear things that really matter.
Deep Silence
allows me to hear my own heart,
the place where God speaks,
the place where the Divine dwells,
path to a clearer light.

Today, the taste for Silence
is becoming lost,
and with it,
the Wisdom of the Ages.
My ears are assaulted by noise
wherever I turn.

I am called to practice Silence
both Interior and Exterior.

Silence is Union with the Divine,
but how am I to hear
that still small voice
of the Divine?

Exterior Silence,
while helpful,
is not essential to my deep inner Silence
where God's voice can be heard.
But it does require
an occasional withdrawal
into that still place within me,
even if only for five or ten minutes.

It is not easy!
Nothing makes as much noise
as my inner voice
which keeps commentaries and discussions
on every conceivable topic.

I know that
in order to be totally oriented to God,
I must be silent.
I must put a stop to inner discussions!

But I know that I cannot do it alone.
My inner voice will never be totally quiet
unless God takes a hand.

It is a Gift.

I can make efforts to attain it,
but I cannot achieve it on my own.

Silence requires Forgetfulness.
I must forget myself for a moment
and listen to The Other,
to the One who is Love.

The paradox is that
even though I cannot achieve it on my own,
I know I must never stop trying.

By continually striving for
Silence,
I am lead deeper and deeper
to where the secret promptings of
the Holy Spirit
are louder and stronger
than the noise of the world.

God spoke only
One Word:
The Son.

It is Spoken
in an Eternal Silence.

Nothing exists
outside this present moment.

I used to think of my lifetime
as a journey from birth to death
with the present moment a single point
on that journey
moving slowly forward.

The past
was the part of the journey
behind that point,
and the future was the part ahead of it.

I have stopped thinking of my life in this way,
finally understanding that this way of thinking
was extremely disempowering.

NOW is all there is.
The past and the future are illusions.
They only exist to the degree
I focus my attention on them right now.

I create the past and the future
by imagining them in the present.

Even I do not exist outside the Now.

It is a radical new way of thinking for me.

Grasping the idea that nothing exists outside
this present moment
has turned my overall approach to life
upside down.

If I am to experience anything in life,
I must create it in this moment.
It must exist in some form right now,
or it doesn't exist at all.

The idea of creating happiness in the future
by constraining myself in the present
was nothing but a fool's errand.

That future would never arrive
as long as I was living in confinement,
in the bushel,
in the here and now.

As I cross
the footbridge of life,
I dare not spend time and energy
wondering what's on the other side,
instead stepping carefully
while enjoying the view
all about me
across the abyss.

To cross,
I have had to leave the past behind,
as the footbridge of life
cannot carry the load
of all I remember or don't.

Unburdened
with past hurts, regrets, sorrows, and sadness,
and
fears, anxieties, and apprehensions about the
future,
I can make the trek across
enjoying each day,
each step.

I discovered
it was time to balance
the masculine and feminine
within our belief systems,
our religious doctrines,
our cultural ethos,
and within myself.

To help achieve this equilibrium,
I focused on the idea of Universal Motherhood
exploring the metaphor of the Mother,
the symbol of the Goddess,
the Wisdom of Sofia,
and the excitement of Women Priests.

I have been enriched
by the archaeological evidence
of ancient Goddesses and their stories.

Through a focus on the feminine,
in and around me,
I have grown in
wisdom,
compassion
and creativity,
gaining a respect for sexuality
as natural and sacred.

I have supported the empowerment of women
celebrating their contribution
to spirituality,
culture and
society.

This focus on the Sacred Feminine
has helped me appreciate the feminine nature
in women
and in men.
Awareness of a Universal Motherhood
has helped me gain respect for the earth
and Mother Nature.

Awareness of the Sacred Feminine
has helped me honor women's bio-physical
and emotional passages through life,
helping me and others
attain healthy self-esteem.

And this awareness helped me find inner
balance and peace,
thereby increasing my respect and tolerance of
others,
promoting greater harmony.

My focus on the feminine
within myself
and in Life
has moved me out of my mind
and into my Heart,
opening me to
Love,
Human and Divine.

By
Being in Love
I become One with God,
BEING-in-Love.

The Pharisees were fervent,
concerned with being absolutely orthodox.
Whenever one is concerned about being right,
some form of "purity code" takes over,
which is largely about rules.
God will love me if I do this
or if I don't do that
appeals to many people,
as it gives a sense of security,
albeit false.

Both Jesus and Paul condemn that mentality,
so common,
even today.

It tends to represent immature religion,
and it cannot get one very far.
It becomes all about naval-gazing,
about how perfect I am
and how terrible other people are,
and then leads to the false conclusion
that I'm better than others
because I don't touch this or eat that.

If people get stuck here,
the purity codes soon morph into debt codes.

It's not just about things that one must do or
must not do,
but debts one must pay to a wrathful God.

It all makes sense inside the small frame of
retributive justice.
It makes no sense inside of love.

Why
did I leave
the safe secure confines
of the One True Church?

Life there
was so straightforward,
clear,
well-defined,
logical,
documented,
explainable.

Life outside the institution
seems so
ambiguous,
unclear,
amorphous,
scary,
undefined.

Life in the Church
was rationally religious,
with life outside,
unreasonably Spiritual
(whatever that is.)

How can I possibly grow
in such an unstructured setting,
without the leadership
of God's intermediaries on earth,
the priests,
showing me the way,
as they did in my youth.

What could possibly make me think
I am not responsible for Jesus' death,
that I am not fallen,
that I am not sinful,
that I do not have to die to reach Heaven,
that God dwells in me,
that men and women are equals,
that gays and lesbians are not
inherently disordered,
that All of Creation is the Incarnation
of God?

Life was so much simpler
within the walls;
Trying to figure these things out for myself,
so difficult.

Church gave me so many answers;
Life outside,
so many Questions.

Church told me
what Jesus really expected of me,
to worship Him every weekend;
I cannot find that expectation on my own
outside the walls.

Outside the Church,
how can I possibly tap into
God's Grace
when Church is the sole official dispenser
of such Grace?

Should we butterflies
try to reverse the process
and become caterpillars again?

Can I crawl back
under the bushel
where it is warm, dark, secure, and safe?

Why did I ever leave?

To find me,
True me,
Child of the <u>unconfined</u> God,
Created in the image and likeness . . .

They convinced me
they were the source
of Light
and that I should not
Venture
(out of the bushel)
into
Darkness.

Despite their dire warnings,
I heeded the call of the Spirit
and
Ventured Out
only to discover
it was darker
IN the bushel
than Out.

The True Source
cannot be confined
to any bushel.

Would I go back
to institutional Catholic Church
if it treated women as equals,
ordaining those seeking ordination?

if it rid the hierarchy
of child-abuse protectors?

if it treated LGBT's
as children of God,
respecting their rights?

if all of its financial dealings
we're transparent and accountable?

if it's hierarchy
was one of Servant Leadership
accountable to the people?

if it fully implemented
All the reforms of Vatican II?

I'd sure be tempted
to return to institutional church,
but honestly might NOT

because its basic redemption theology
is all wrong.

I am evolving,
but not fallen,
and I do not see the Creator
as one who required the death of Jesus
to Love me.
I did not kill Jesus,
who died at the hands of
the hierarchy of His day,
not because of any of my failings.

Jesus needed no intermediary
between Him and His Creator
and did not establish one
between me and my Creator.

I joyfully seek out anyone
that can help
with my growth and transformation,
but likely not
an institution created for the benefit of
its own hierarchy,
and one more in love with
its own rules and regulations,
rites and rituals,
than with God.

Why go back?
I'll just keep going outward,
forward,
upward.

We Can Learn from the Buddhists

<u>Ego</u>

One of the greatest weaknesses
of modern Christianity
has been the focus on the individual.
This comes more from our individualistic culture
than from Christianity itself.

Though we focus on personal
(often translated as sexual) sin,
the idea of sin within the Hebrew Bible was
more corporate.
There was more of an interdependent,
community culture.

We've also focused too much on personal
salvation
or a "personal relationship with Jesus Christ,"
which has also led to
bastardized interpretations
as the false gospel of personal salvation.

In Buddhist practices,
one must learn to let the self die, in a manner of
speaking,

in order to create a deeper,
more meaningful relationship
and interdependence with others
and the rest of creation.
This is actually more consistent
with ancient Jewish
and Christian thought
than our modern, egocentric version
of Christianity.

Seeking Wisdom, not Knowledge

Many, growing up, were taught
to know the Bible inside and out
— or at least to memorize it —
to be ready to argue with anyone
who refuted it in any way.
Meanwhile they didn't spend much,
if any, time
actually experiencing the "real world."

Though our present culture values
amassing knowledge, or expertise,
it actually does very little to prepare us
to *live* in a Christ-like way
beyond the church walls.

Wisdom, unlike knowledge,
comes as a byproduct of lived experience.
Something happens, and as often as not,
we screw up.
Then we reflect, learn,
and change our attitudes or behaviors
moving forward.

Christianity, however, too often teaches us
to entrench ourselves in self-righteousness,
seeking instead to change others
to be more like us.
(God forbid we would be changed by
someone who isn't a Christian.)
But true wisdom means
learning and being affected by
all of our experiences,
and using that wisdom as an opportunity
to do and be better in the future.

Right-Heartedness Over Right Belief

When someone joins a Christian church,
or before they get baptized
or commit their lives to Christ,
we inevitably ask them with three telltale words:
"DO YOU BELIEVE..."

But Jesus didn't ask people what they believed,
or to recite some creed
before following him
or going and doing for others
what he did for them.
He was more concerned with
the nature of their hearts
than any claim of belief.

This is where a fundamental tenet of Buddhism
serves us very well.
We're taught that right hearts
lead to right thoughts,
and this, in turn, leads to right action.
But it all begins with
the orientation of our hearts,
how we see, receive and respond to the world.
We're not sent out into the world so much to
coerce people
into like-thought;
rather, we're charged with going out
and offering ourselves fully and sacrificially
in humble service to others,
regardless of who they are,
what they believe
or what the result might be for us.

Impermanence

We seem to become pretty fixated
on some false correlation
between our faithfulness
and the financial health
of our churches and denominations.

We know we're doing God's work if our
churches are full,
budgets are met
and we can hand off
a healthy institutional legacy
to those who come after us.

But Jesus preached
the destruction of the temple
not just to freak people out;
he was warning them not to cling too tightly
to all the trappings of religion around them
that would inevitably crumble and fail.

We can learn much
from the Buddhist artistic discipline
of creating mandalas.

These elaborate sand-art designs
sometimes take weeks or more to make,
with several monks attending to them
many hours each day.
And though our instinct is generally to preserve
and even defend something beautiful,
the mandala is intentionally destroyed
not long after it is finished.

The sand is returned to the earth
and the only remaining impression of the
mandala
is in our consciousness.
It's a humbling exercise in letting go,
one from which we can learn a great deal.

Care for All Creation

We Christians have been greatly affected by
the industrial revolution
in ways that have negatively impacted
our relationship
with the rest of creation.

This, combined with an over-emphasis
of disdain
for our own bodies and sexual identities,
has created a sense of disembodiment
that also causes us to feel
less interdependent on each other
and less dependent on all of nature.

The notion of dominionism falsely teaches
within some Christian circles
that the planet is ours to use as we please.

And some even go so far
as to suggest that
anything we can do to help
hasten the end-times
gets us that much closer to heralding God's
kingdom on earth.

Buddhism, however, teaches simplicity, humility
and intentional care for all of creation.
Practices of mindfulness and humility
help us loosen our grasp on personal desire
and avail ourselves to the excesses and
insensitivity of our habits.

When we regain a healthier sense
of our own places
within a much larger,
very delicate ecosystem,
we not only treat our surroundings
with more care;
we treat ourselves
with greater care as well.

Much to Learn.

Though some thought
I was too driven by my Anger
at how the hierarchs had corrupted
my church,
it was as much my Grief
at the loss of all that I thought church should
be.

Nonetheless,
I took to heart the question
of being controlled by my Anger
rather than
my life-guiding principal of Love.

In the process,
with the help of people
like Anthony DeMello, Richard Rohr, and Henri
Nouwen,
and friends who were concerned about me,
I came to the realization that
the failures of institutional Catholicism
need have nothing at all
to do with
my own Spiritual Growth and fulfillment.

When I came to the realization that
the perverse actions of the hierarchy
were irrelevant
to my True Faith,
I was able to *Let Go*
of a driving need to speak out
and write about the abuse.

In *Letting Go,*
I discovered
just how much of my time and attention
were being devoted to institutional failure
by the size of the vacuum
left behind in me.

*I was, in fact, squandering too much energy
on something irrelevant to my own
Spiritual Growth.*

Though the vacuum left behind in me
is uncomfortable and achy,
I know that just as Nature abhors a vacuum
and rushes to fill it,
so the Holy Spirit will on Her time and in Her Way
fill mine.

. . . to Live the Questions

If I'm to Live the Questions
I don't need to pray for
clarity or insight
in my life.

I need to pray for
Confusion.

After 78+ years
of trying to Learn Life's Lessons,
I am more than willing to tell people
I just do not know,
I'm not sure.

Despite that willingness
to try and dwell in the ambiguity of life,
at times and much to my regret,
I take refuge in
an answer.

Thank God,
the call to befriend and embrace
Mystery
stays with me.

Thank God,
life does not ever let me completely escape
Confusion.

Thank God,
the Holy Spirit reveals to me
Uncertainty after Uncertainty after Uncertainty.

I will continue to strive to
avoid the arrogance of certainty
and its momentary security.

I have no idea where I am going
and rather than trying to figure it out,

Dear God,
simply help me to trust that
You will never leave me alone.

Proof

Made in the USA
Charleston, SC
24 October 2015